D0491996

GIVE ME EVERYTHING YOU HAVE

GIVE ME EVERYTHING YOU HAVE

On Being Stalked

James Lasdun

JONATHAN CAPE
LONDON

Published by Jonathan Cape 2013

2 4 6 8 10 9 7 5 3 1

Author's Note: This is a true story, but various names, places and details have been changed.
As the reader will come to understand, the claims and allegations made by the woman I call Nasreen are
presented purely as her assertions, and are most certainly not intended to reflect the actual truth about
any person.

First published in the United States in 2013 by
Farrar, Strauss and Giroux, New York

First published in Great Britain in 2013 by
Jonathan Cape
Random House, 20 Vauxhall Bridge Road,
London SW1V 2SA

www.vintage-books.co.uk

Addresses for companies within The Random House Group Limited can be found at:
www.randomhouse.co.uk/offices.htm

The Random House Group Limited Reg. No. 954009

A CIP catalogue record for this book is available from the British Library

ISBN 9780224096621

The Random House Group Limited supports the Forest Stewardship Council® (FSC®),
the leading international forest-certification organisation. Our books carrying the FSC label
are printed on FSC®-certified paper. FSC is the only forest-certification scheme supported by
the leading environmental organisations, including Greenpeace. Our paper procurement
policy can be found at www.randomhouse.co.uk/environment

Part I

Nasreen

A young man on a journey comes across a corpse at the edge of a village. On enquiring why the corpse has not been buried, he is told that the dead man was in debt and that his creditors are refusing permission for the burial to take place until the debts have been paid. The young man, though not rich, immediately pays the debts and the burial goes forward.

That night the dead man comes to thank him. As a token of his gratitude he offers to accompany the young man on his travels and give him the benefit of the supernatural powers death has conferred on him. His only condition is that everything they gain on their adventures be divided equally between them. The young man agrees and the two set off together. All goes well for a year, with treasure after treasure falling into their hands and each of them taking an equal share.

Then one day they meet a woman, young and attractive. And now all of a sudden the men are confronted by an apparently insurmountable problem: how to divide the woman in two.

I read this folk tale at university, where it made a strong impression on me. For many years I kept it in mind as a possible basis for a story, but I could never think of a way to use it and after a while it began to fade from me. I forgot which book I'd read it in, I forgot the details of the adventures the two men have together before they meet the woman, and then I even forgot how they solved the problem of dividing the woman between them.

It was after the attacks on the World Trade Center that I came across the story again. I was trying to track down an aside on Islam in my old Penguin edition of Claude Lévi-Strauss's *Tristes Tropiques* when I saw a passage I must have marked when I first read the book, thirty years ago. It was the story I had forgotten: a version of what is apparently a universal folk-tale motif, known as 'The Grateful Corpse'. It didn't, as it turned out, contain any details of the two men's adventures before they meet the woman, so on that score my memory hadn't, after all, failed me. But it did resolve the question of how to divide the woman in two. It turns out she is bewitched: half woman, half demon. The dead man is interested only in her diabolic aspect and accepts this for his share, leaving a sane and companionable human being for the hero to marry.

In the fall of 2003 I taught a fiction workshop in the graduate writing programme at a place I'll call Morgan College, in New York City. I live upstate, but my wife and I once lived in Greenwich Village, and we'd held on to our rent-stabilised one-bedroom apartment, sharing it with a subtenant from Baltimore who used it only on weekends. The arrangement made it possible for me to take jobs like this in the city.

Among the students in my class was a woman I'll call Nasreen. She was in her thirties, quiet and reserved. Her work didn't come up for discussion until a few weeks into the semester and I didn't notice much about her before then, except that she sat at the back of the room rather than at the large table that I and most of the students sat around – shy perhaps, or aloof, or a bit of both.

When her turn came, she handed in the opening chapter of a novel. It was set in Tehran in the seventies, during the last days of the Shah, and followed the lives of several members of a well-off family close to the Shah's inner circle. The ambition – to tell a story with history and politics in it as well as a large-scale family drama – was quickly apparent. Even more so was the quality of the writing. There are seldom more than a couple of students in any workshop who seem natural writers, and they aren't hard to spot. It was evident to me, after a few paragraphs, that Nasreen was one of them. Her language was clear and vigorous, with a distinct fiery expressiveness in the more dramatic passages that made it a positive pleasure to read. I was extremely impressed.

Although I have taught on and off for twenty years, I've never actually taken a creative-writing class myself, never had my material 'workshopped', as the term goes. When I try to imagine what it might be like, it seems to me that it must be a powerful and unsettling experience: a miniature version of the whole process of bringing out a book, with the editing, publishing, reviewing and sales all jumbled up and compressed into a single tumultuous half-hour. There you sit, listening to a roomful of people appraising something born in the innermost regions of your psyche and brought forth by efforts that probably stretched you to the limits of your abilities. These ten or fifteen pages are who you are as a writer, for now – fully exposed – and the discussion is going to have a highly charged impact on you. Whatever the general verdict, the chances are you're going to come out feeling overwhelmed, whether by euphoria or by despair.

The class's response to Nasreen's chapter was favourable, though perhaps not as warmly so as I'd expected. I spoke last, as I usually do, and it's possible that this slight lack of warmth made me more emphatically enthusiastic than I might have been otherwise. I don't remember what I said, but I do remember a shift in the atmosphere as I spoke: an air of faintly sardonic attentiveness settling on the students as they sat listening to my words of praise. I didn't interpret this as envy so much as the reluctant registering of the thought that the class, which had seemed to be of fairly uniform ability till now, was after all going to have a star, and that this was going to be Nasreen. Not necessarily a calamitous thought, but one that had to be adjusted to in some way.

Nasreen herself appeared pleased with the way things went, though contrary to my general hypothesis, she didn't seem overwhelmed, and she certainly didn't effuse in the way some students do after a positive response. I suspected she was confident in her abilities, no doubt glad to have had them recognised, but too much her own critic to be all that affected by other people's views. And this too, this unflustered reaction of hers, seemed to me the mark of a real writer.

She turned in two more chapters that semester. Both reaffirmed my sense of her talent, though they also made it apparent that she had set herself a difficult challenge with her large cast of characters and her decision to accompany the action with dense historical analysis. The shifts in point of view were coming a little too thick and fast for comfort, and she hadn't found a way of incorporating the history into the story, so that lumps of it sat here and there like undigested portions of an encyclopedia.

As her thesis adviser, I met with her a few times during office hours towards the end of that term, and we talked about these and other matters. Though she still gave the impression of keeping a part of herself averted, she was a little more forthcoming in private than she was in the classroom. She revealed a self-deprecating sense of humour, laughing at her folly – as she claimed to see it – in embarking on this large enterprise. And in her quiet way she also seemed curious about me: asking how I'd become a writer, what I was working on now, who my favourite novelists were.

As I'd assumed, the family in her novel was based on her own family, who had fled Iran for the States at the time of the 1979 revolution, when she was a child. I remembered following those events myself: the Ayatollah's thunderous speeches from exile, the toppling of the Shah and his SAVAK security apparatus, the massive street demonstrations, the first intimations of what a radical Islamic regime was going to look like as the decrees went out concerning books, alcohol, dress. I was twenty, and this was the first revolution I had been old enough to pay serious attention to. London, where I was living, was full of Iranian exiles and refugees, among them some family friends who had taken my parents around the monuments of Isfahan and Persepolis a few years earlier. The trip had made a strong impression on my father, an architect, and, as always happened when something caught his imagination, a vibrant link had established itself between the subject and our entire household. Photos appeared on the shelves: stone lions, blue domes, latticed archways standing against desert skies. Books on Mughal architecture lay open on the side tables. A small fragment of a column that my father had pillaged and smuggled home was set up in a lit niche in our living room. Since then, even though I hadn't been on the trip, I have felt an interest – or, more accurately, a kind of latent, hereditary entitlement to be interested – in Persian culture.

All of which is to say that as Nasreen talked about her family, memories stirred in me, and in a minor way I felt a connection to her as a person.

Her appearance conveyed, over time, the same undemonstrative confidence as her manner in class. She wore jeans that looked expensively soft and faded, and a brown, waist-length jacket, at once military and feminine in its cut, that emphasised her aura of self-containment. Her dark hair was usually pinned up – neatly, but with a few strands falling loose. Her face, fine-boned, with delicately interlocking features, had the same sallow olive complexion as my own.

The line of her brown eyes had the slight upward curve at the outer corners that puts one – or anyway me – in mind of the scimitar-like flourishes of Arabic script.

During one of our conversations she mentioned a fiancé. I was struck by this: not the fact itself so much as the word. Though not exactly old-fashioned, it suggested a very different order of relationship from the casual hook-up that I assumed (based on their writing) to be the norm among the students. It also accorded with my sense of her as a writer. There was something novelistic in the attitude to life it evoked: a suggestion of build, coherence, strong emotion maximised by strong formal design. In short, I approved.

She was graduating that summer, and since I wasn't going to be teaching then, I didn't expect to see or hear from her again. To the extent that I thought of her after our final meeting, it was as someone gone into a sunlit future of artistic and personal fulfilment.

Two years passed, during which I heard nothing from Nasreen. And then, in December 2005, she emailed to say she had completed a draft of her novel and to ask if I would read it.

I'd just finished teaching at Morgan College for the year and had arranged things so that I wouldn't have to teach again until the following fall. Much as I'd admired Nasreen's work, I didn't want to spend time reading or thinking about any student's or former student's writing during this period, and, as politely as I could, I declined her request. I did, however, feel confident enough to offer to recommend her to my agent – I'll call her Janice Schwartz – who was looking for clients and who I thought might be interested in Nasreen's work.

Nasreen thanked me politely for the offer, saying that she already had some tentative interest from other agents, as well as one or two editors, and asking my advice on how to proceed, in terms of showing the book around.

An amicable email correspondence developed over the next few weeks. At that time I wasn't yet keeping copies of every email Nasreen sent, but I did save some of them. For quite a while they remain unremarkable. She asks how I think she should handle this or that nibble of interest from this or that agent or editor. She mentions a boring administrative job she has taken at a college in the city. She recommends a CD by a Persian-American musician friend of hers. She debates whether or not to take me up on my offer to put her in touch with my agent. The emails are chatty and, given Nasreen's quietness in class, surprisingly exuberant in style. The ones I sent back are a little terser, though friendly, with plenty of encouragement about the book and some minor attempts at humour: 'my commiserations about having to get an office job. With luck you'll soon be able to buy the office.'

On 13 January 2006, she grumbles about an agent who has passed on the book and forwards me the rejection letter, saying she has now decided that she would like to send the book to my own agent, Janice, and concluding: 'sorry to bother you with my neuroses and personal literary troubles. I hope you are well and that we can share a cup of coffee after all this works out (or doesn't work out) or something.' I commiserate further, suggest one or two things to say in her letter to Janice, and agree that it would be nice to meet for coffee sometime. On 20 January she asks why I am no longer teaching and offers me 'exorbitant sums of money to be my adviser again'. Joking, I assume, or maybe only half joking, since she adds: 'would you be interested?' I thank her but explain that I simply don't have the time.

As winter progresses, her notes become steadily warmer, more gossipy and inquisitive; full of questions about me, my past, my writing habits and my family, along with ruefully amused gripes about prevaricating agents, the tedium of her job, and so on. She asks what I'm writing and I tell her I'm doing a screen adaptation of my wife's uncompleted novel. Again she asks me to work with her on the book; again I decline. Sometimes she drops in a more personal disclosure, alluding, for instance, to the fact that she has broken off her engagement. All she offers by way of explanation is 'I can't marry A—', the effect of which is to add a note of stoical sacrifice to the cluster of other sentiments she had prompted in me by her use of the word 'fiancé'.

My own emails back, while still brief, grew more friendly and unguarded as the weeks passed. Not being her 'professor', or anyone else's, at that period, I had been happily discarding the rather formal, aloof persona in which I tend to armour myself for my forays into the academic world. Consequently I had begun to experience a shift in my feelings about Nasreen, from the slightly harassed sense of obligation I'd started off with to a more human, straightforward feeling of affection.

In the secluded life I lead – near Woodstock, New York, but out in the country – I don't often meet new people, much less anyone I'm likely to have enough in common with for a real friendship to develop. On the rare occasions when such a person does appear in my life, I tend to be eagerly friendly. Jim Morrison's line *I need a brand-new friend* is often in my mind, and as my correspondence with Nasreen continued, I began to think of her as something like that: a brand-new friend. That she was younger than me, a woman and Iranian were all things that gave the prospect of this friendship a certain appealing novelty (most of my friends are middle-aged Western men like myself), but the main thing (given that any relationship between us was likely to be of a purely epistolary nature) was that she was a fellow writer whose work I genuinely admired and who seemed to enjoy being in communication with me. I assumed she felt something similar about me.

Still, at a certain point I realised I was being flirted with. Not, I felt, with any serious underlying intent: more in deference to some sort of vague convention she seemed to adhere to, concerning the correct tone for a correspondence between a youngish woman and an older man whose support she considers worth securing. ('Older man' . . . the first time I've used that phrase about myself. Among the other effects of my encounter with Nasreen is the fact that I no longer think of myself as young.) That this convention, as I perceived it, should be somewhat old-fashioned seemed in keeping with the rest of her character. There was something of another era in the way she presented herself in this first phase of emails; even of another culture. And in fact when, much later, I came across an account of all the precise gradations of flirtatiousness and coquettishness once recognised in Persian society, each with its own word – *eshveh, kereshmeh, naz* – I wondered if I hadn't been at the receiving end of some late, anachronistic flowering of that ancient tradition.

In one email, for instance, she wrote that a classmate of hers in the workshop I'd taught – I'll call him Glen – had told her that he and some of the other students had thought that she and I were having an affair. This didn't seem plausible, and I assumed she was either making it up or else massively exaggerating some remark made by Glen as a joke. Either way, the intent seemed to be to introduce, under cover of mildly salacious gossip, a notion that I might (so I imagine her thinking) find amusing, perhaps titillating, perhaps even tempting.

I don't mind being flirted with – in fact I quite like it – and although I made no conscious effort to encourage this development, I didn't feel any pressing need to discourage it either. To the comment about Glen I responded: 'That's funny about Glen. He's obviously a born writer,' which seemed to me a way of maintaining the pleasantly light-hearted tone of our correspondence while tactfully keeping my distance.

A couple of weeks later she remembers, or purports to remember, my having 'snapped' at her once in class – a reproach that I also sense to be mildly flirtatious, inviting me, as it does, to sweeten the alleged sting. Again, in my reply, I see myself trying to keep the playful tone alive without actually rising to the bait: 'Snapped at you, huh?' I say. 'That really is a little hard to believe. Are you sure I didn't just push you to declare an opinion on something? (I remember you being rather reticent.)' I then add, sententiously though, in the light of the catastrophe that later unfolded, with odd clairvoyance: 'As George Eliot said, the last thing we learn in life is our effect on other people.'

In March, after several near misses with other agents and editors, she finally sent the manuscript to my agent, Janice. I felt there was a good chance that Janice would want to sign her up. Aside from the quality of the material, everything about Nasreen's profile – age, gender, nationality – seemed to me to make her an eminently marketable prospect. Still, I didn't want to raise her hopes, and I was careful not to sound too confident.

Janice happened to be travelling at this time and was slow getting to the book. The delay, along with the fact that I was the one responsible for this introduction, made me feel under more of an obligation than I had before. Reversing my earlier position, I offered to read the first section of the novel myself, so as to be able to be more specific in my recommendation to Janice. I was planning to be in New York for a couple of days in late April, and we arranged that Nasreen would give me the pages when I came down. A date and time were set for the handover, and a cafe in the Village selected for the location. As the day for this meeting approached, it took on a vaguely fateful character, at least in my mind, what with the some-how momentous question of how Janice was going to respond to the book hanging over it, not to mention the cumulative effect of Nasreen's emails, which were now coming rather frequently, so that I was beginning to feel a little saturated by her, or by the thought of her.

Among these recent emails was one containing a strange photograph of herself, taken in her twenties. It was just of her face, and it was exposed in such a way that almost nothing showed except the curving lines of her eyes and mouth and a few wisps of hair, making her look like a ghost. I wasn't sure whether sending me this fell into the category of flirting or was just a normal thing for people a decade younger than myself to do, people who had instantly embraced all the conveniences of Internet communication, as she had (she was always sending attachments and links), instead of being daunted by them, as I was. Whatever the case, the incandescent face of that photograph had supplanted what remained of my somewhat hazy memory of her actual appearance, and when I arrived at the cafe for our meeting it took me a few seconds to realise that the dark-haired woman in her mid-thirties wearing sensible office clothes and talking with a harried expression on her cell phone by the counter was in fact Nasreen. She closed the phone and, after a slightly awkward greeting, we went to sit at the back of the cafe, by a window opening onto a stone courtyard.

The meeting, which lasted about half an hour, had a muffled, muted quality – oddly so, given the build-up. Despite her extravagant loquaciousness as an emailer, Nasreen was even quieter in person than I remembered her. Not that she wasn't perfectly pleasant, but there was something cancelled or hidden, somehow, about her bearing; a strange irreality in her presence across from me at our lacquered pine table, as if she were absent in all but the most literal, mechanical sense.

Our conversation was friendly enough but desultory. She spoke caustically about her family, some in New York, some in California, giving an impression that her artistic ambitions and unsettled life had cast her in the role of black sheep – not shunned exactly, but clearly not approved of. There was money, she implied, but not much of it flowing in her direction. Picking up on this rueful note, I mentioned a problem of my own that had just arisen, concerning our apartment. Our subtenant, the woman from Baltimore, had called the day before to say she was buying a studio and no longer needed to share with us. This was a blow, as it had been extremely hard to find a tenant whose needs dovetailed as conveniently with ours as hers did, and I seriously doubted whether we would be able to find anyone else. Even if we did, there was a danger that the management company that had recently bought the building and installed an office inside would notice the new face, put two and two together, and realise we were subletting against the rules of our lease. We couldn't afford to keep the place unless we shared it, so we were looking at the prospect of losing our foothold in New York.

All of this had been weighing on me since our tenant's call, and it was what came naturally to mind as something to talk about in response to Nasreen's comments about her own financial troubles. Nasreen listened politely, but I had the impression that she wasn't taking much of it in.

We finished our coffees and left the cafe. Outside, we walked in the same direction for a couple of blocks. Nasreen lit a cigarette and smoked it beside me, silent except for the light clopping of her heels on the sidewalk. She seemed frail, I thought; possibly a little stressed. At the corner where our ways parted she gave me the manuscript, and, with a quick kiss on the cheek, we said goodbye.

I had some anxiety about reading the manuscript. What if, despite the great promise of the drafts I'd seen two years earlier, she had somehow botched things? I know from experience how easy it is to lose the thread of a narrative. One wrong turn and you can end up spending months or even years in a wilderness of futile and wasted effort. Or what if I simply didn't like it as much as I had? What would I say? How might she take it? These manuscripts are a dense embodiment of their creators' deepest drives and ambitions. Large forces circulate around them. They come into your hands, as a reader, charged with volatile potentialities of trust and suspicion, hope and fear, friendship and eternal enmity. This too I know from experience, and I opened the padded envelope with a familiar sense of foreboding.

I needn't have worried. The writing was as good as I remembered it: strong sentences confidently evoking the epic setting of Tehran on the brink of revolution, a sharply drawn cast of characters with an interestingly unbalanced heroine at the centre, and a storyline of love tangles and political power struggles that seemed to be plunging swiftly forward under its own effortless momentum. I had criticisms, mainly about the essayistic passages, which still felt extraneous to the narrative, but this seemed something a good editor could easily remedy, and in general I felt entirely vindicated in my earlier enthusiasm.

I emailed Nasreen, detailing my responses and attaching a copy of an email I'd sent Janice, reiterating my support.

As far as I understood, the rest of the novel existed only in very rough draft, and I do remember being concerned that, since even this first section needed another pass, Janice might feel it was too early to commit herself as the agent. My own view was that the forcefulness of the writing, evident from the first page, was sufficient guarantee that a good book was going to emerge sooner or later. For me, at that time, the definition of a writer was very simply, as some critic put it, someone who has 'an interesting way with words'. Do the sentences engage you? Cast a spell over you? Make you want to read on? If so, that's enough, regardless of the story itself. If not, no amount of socially, politically, or otherwise 'relevant' material is going to make a difference. I don't feel so sure of this any more (I don't feel so sure of anything any more), but even at the time I was aware that not everyone shared this rather cavalier way of judging a piece of writing. And I could certainly imagine that from the point of view of an agent debating whether or not to take on a first novel – the hardest kind of book to sell – an 'interesting way with words' might not be quite enough of an incentive.

Janice was impressed enough to invite Nasreen in for a meeting. By all accounts the meeting was pleasant and positive, but in the end, as I'd feared, she decided the book was still too far from completion to take on for the moment. She did, however, recommend Nasreen to a friend of hers – I'll call her Paula Kurwen – who worked as a freelance editor. I'd never met Paula, but I knew she had a good reputation. She liked the manuscript enough to feel able to help shape it, and very soon Nasreen sent me an enthusiastic email saying that the two of them were working productively together. It wasn't quite the same as being taken on by an agent, but it was probably the best outcome that could be hoped for at this stage in the book's development. At any rate it was certainly a step in the right direction, and I was glad to have been able to play a part.

In June I had to do some travelling – to London and back, then on to Los Angeles. As I had some time in between the two journeys, I decided to make the trip to LA by train, on one of the double-decker Amtrak Superliners that begin in Chicago and cross the country in leisurely, old-fashioned style, with glass-walled observation cars, dining compartments and private 'roomettes'. The journey takes three days from Chicago, and I planned to break it up for an extra night in New Mexico. In the uneventful life I lead, this expedition constituted major news, and I mentioned it in an email to Nasreen, along with the other, more humdrum highlights of that spring, such as the escape of our pet cockatiel and my project to cover the walk-ways in my vegetable garden with stone.

Nasreen seemed to enjoy these little bulletins from my life and often wrote back about them with an astringent insight that I appreciated. About my stonework, for instance, a project that had begun to obsess me, she joked that I was building myself a 'fortress' – an image that struck me as peculiarly accurate. (It was also, in its quick, confident transformation of my flat walkways into a solid building, characteristic of the verve and directness I admired in her writing.)

But her response to the news of my impending train trip was a little different. That it fell into the category of flirtation was nothing new in itself, and no doubt it was meant no more seriously than any of its predecessors, but the actual content seemed a significant escalation of the terms: an attempt to insert herself into my mind in an unambiguously erotic light. She was proposing to smuggle herself into my roomette for the journey, and wanted to know when my train was leaving. I didn't respond, but at this point I began to realise that something more explicitly discouraging than a mere tactful silence was going to be required of me.

Around this time, my wife and I (but I don't like that Buckingham Palace phrase: I'll call her K——, which is the initial of her real name, though not the name she uses) – K—— and I – sent out a proposal for a book we wanted to write. Years earlier, before we had children, we had written a book called *Walking and Eating in Tuscany and Umbria*. It had been a modest success, and now, with our kids aged seven and eleven, we'd decided it would be interesting to do another one, *en famille*, this time in Provence. I began my cross-country train journey on 8 June and flew back from LA ten days later. Soon after my return, a publisher made an offer for our book. The advance would allow us to live in Provence for four months, long enough to cover all the more promising-looking corners of the region, and we accepted. Our plan was to leave early the following year.

I mentioned this to Nasreen in my next email and made a point of emphasising the family aspect of it all. She didn't respond directly, but a week later she sent me an email in which she described a short story that a former member of her workshop – I'll call her Elaine – had just sent her, about an American woman who seduces an Arab man. The email had the slight incoherence of something written under great emotional pressure, and culminated in an assertion that Elaine's story was a thinly disguised account of a real affair; that the American woman in it was Elaine herself and the Arab man was, of all people, me. In effect Nasreen appeared to be reproaching me for rejecting her as a lover and accusing me of favouritism by having bestowed my attentions on another student.

The bizarreness of this scenario – bizarre to me at least: I'm not used to being regarded as some kind of pasha surrounded by desirous women – disturbed me almost as much as the accusation itself. I'd made it clear, or thought I had, that I was happily married and not interested in having an affair, but apparently it needed to be spelled out. I hated having to do this: it seemed a retreat from the living connection of a real relationship with another human being into the safe, deadening geometry of convention.

On 30 June I wrote back:

```
I don't really know what any of this is about—I haven't
read [Elaine's] story and for the record haven't ever had
an affair with a student or ex student and am not about to
start now. I like your writing and want to help, but I
don't want to be a figment in anyone's private fantasies,
or at least I don't particularly want to know about it if
I am. I guess it's possible that I've been taking your
emails in a less serious spirit than they were intended—in
which case apologies. Anyway, I do think you're very
talented, which is why I tried to get Janice to take you
```

on. I'm sorry she didn't, but I still have high hopes for
your book, and I think you should concentrate on getting
it done as quickly as possible.

Her initial reaction was to remain curiously insistent, and a
couple of days later I felt compelled to send a follow-up:

I don't know what to tell you Nasreen. I guess on the rare
occasions when I like someone's writing I tend to feel an
affinity with them, an openness to friendship. Forgive me
if this has read differently to you; that certainly
wasn't my intention. I'm sorry things have come to this
and I don't want to upset you, but I really am extremely
happily married and I don't particularly want to go on
having this correspondence any more if it's going to be
like this.

I'd resigned myself to the ending of this friendship, but a week
later Nasreen sent a lucid, gracious email, from which the following
statements merit quoting, if only for their relevance to what came
later:

. . . I'm not used to having men lend me support, help or
friendship without any sort of amorous or sexual
intentions. I didn't really think that's where you were
taking this very benign relationship of ours. And in a
sense I do love you and am in love with you—but mainly
because you've given me hope that there are some "normal"
men out there . . .
    I'm sorry if I got screwy on you. Please laugh. I have
to, or I'll be so embarrassed (I am: trying to
rationalize it as all writers are insane) . . .

I'm also glad you're so respectful of your wife and
family that you made me shut up. It was good
therapy . . .

For a couple of months following this, our correspondence resumes its breezy, amicable tone. Nasreen sends progress reports on
her work with Paula, which appears to be going well. She adopts a
puppy and sends pictures. She jokes about her awful new boss. She
debates whether to escape the nightmare of Bush's America and live
abroad. She also starts writing about other men she is interested in – 'I
think I've found my next prey . . . He's a very handsome writer . . . He
may have a girlfriend but that's no matter . . .' – reassigning me, so it
appears, from 'prey' to something more like confidant.

In August she mentions being at a party where my father was
being discussed. My father had designed several well-known public
buildings in England, and had been knighted for his work. This connection of mine to a 'Sir' amused Nasreen no end. She took to calling me 'Sir James' in some of her emails, sometimes varying it with
'St. James', or plain 'Sir'. The comedies of being English, of being a
faithful ('saintly') husband and of being a teacher (that ridiculous
object of schoolgirl crushes) were all compressed into these designa-
tions, and through them I could sense, again, a mind akin to my
own, someone for whom words were a source of primal delight.
Much more than me, in fact, she was someone whom words 'stuck
to' in odd ways, becoming an elemental part of the reality she in-
habited. Often she wrote things in her emails that appeared almost
nonsensical until, days later, I would suddenly grasp what was being
alluded to by the puzzling word or phrase. An example: several
months after our meeting in New York, she ended an email: 'I'm
s'nice, aren't I?' The abbreviation seemed just throwaway odd, but
later I happened to pass the cafe where we'd met (I hadn't known its
name, only the location) and I saw that it was called 'sNice – my first

20

indication that Nasreen had been less 'absent' on this occasion than I had thought. More significant perhaps, that word 'fortress', which had touched such a nerve in me, turned out (and this is a measure of my comparative carelessness with words, even my own) to be a sly recycling of something I myself had written, namely this phrase in a novel of mine, *The Horned Man* (later emails confirmed she had read it closely), where my protagonist talks about his unsatisfactory love life: 'I had come to realise that I no longer wanted a "lover" or a "girlfriend", that I wanted a *wife*. I wanted something durable about me – a fortress and a sanctuary.'

My point here is partly to illustrate my continued feeling of affinity with Nasreen, my sense of being on her wavelength, sometimes uncannily so; but also to introduce the idea of a certain porousness in her sense of who she actually was. Harmlessly manifested here, but foreshadowing a more troubling, and then threatening, amorphousness of identity that began emerging not long after.

Staying, for a moment, with this particular line of development, the next discernible phase came on 20 September, in an email in which Nasreen included, in its entirety, a private email to her from another former classmate, attacking various other students in their workshop. We all know, of course, that email is not a strictly private form of communication, but even so, and even though Nasreen acknowledged something dubious about copying the email ('it may be unethical of me to show you this'), I sensed, for the first time, a lack of scruple that I hadn't previously suspected. Obviously my own use of Nasreen's emails in this narrative lays me open to the charge of hypocrisy here. I don't believe I'm guilty of that, but rather than explain or justify myself at this point, I must simply ask for the reader's patience. This is a complicated story and we are still only in the preamble.

Later that same day, as if sensing my misgivings, Nasreen emailed again: 'I hope you know that I don't share your emails/thoughts with anyone.' Somehow this assurance had the opposite of its intended effect. I didn't think I'd sent anything I'd be embarrassed about other people reading, but it bothered me that the very concept of 'sharing' or not sharing my emails with other people should exist in her mind, and it had a distinctly cooling effect on my desire to communicate with her.

Around this time, Nasreen began dropping allusions to Rilke in some of her emails, especially to his figure of the Angel, from the *Duino Elegies*, with whom she seemed to identify. I remembered this Angel, from my own reading of Rilke, as a force of violently transformative power, invoked by mortals at their peril. Intrigued that Nasreen should see herself in such a figure, I'd reread Heidegger's essay on Rilke, 'What Are Poets For?', vaguely remembering that he discusses the Angel there, which he does, at some length. 'The Angel of the *Elegies*,' he writes, 'is that being who assures the recognition of a higher order of reality in the invisible . . .' Given the tone of her later emails, I imagine it was this aspect, this godlike gift for revelation, that Nasreen had in mind in adopting the Angel as one her many private personae. But what struck me most, rereading the essay, was another aspect, touched on only in passing by Heidegger, but curiously apposite: 'This being,' goes this other description (and it was one I was to recall many times in the months and years that followed), '*for whom borderlines and differences . . . hardly exist any longer . . .*'

Even before these melting and merging tendencies of Nasreen's began manifesting themselves, my emails to her had been growing shorter and more guarded. The reason for this was partly the overwhelming quantity of emails Nasreen was now sending me – often several a day – and partly a resurgence of that once flattering but now merely disconcerting flirtatiousness.

Again, this flirtatiousness was expressed playfully at first, under the sign of its own acknowledged futility. But over the weeks it grew

22

more insistent, as if my rejection had given it licence to evolve in a kind of negative space, feeding off its own extravagance, as in certain kinds of love poetry where the emotion grows fantastical in proportion to the strength of the resistance it meets. 7 September: 'You don't love me at all anymore do you, James?' 19 September: 'Just a sip of water from the Zamzam well that overfloweth despite the disappearance of the Son of Thunder' (in addition to 'Sir' I was now the 'Son of Thunder' and sometimes 'Mr Thunder'). 20 September: 'James, you should marry me and I'll support all of the Lasduns . . .'

I began to feel that I was becoming more a source of frustration for Nasreen than anything else, and that since I couldn't be what she wanted me to be, I should withdraw altogether. On the other hand, a part of me still clung to the idea of her as a fascinating new friend, not, after all, any crazier than some of my other writer friends, and one who seemed to find me useful as a sounding board for her own evolving vocabulary of symbols and metaphors. Having formally severed (from my end at least) any erotic current between us, I was ready to assume the role of one of those avuncular, rather eunuchy types who crop up now and then in literature: a critic-mentor figure enlisted by some gifted younger writer he's had the good or bad luck to cross paths with. (I'd have found it unimaginable to be anything other than the 'gifted younger writer' myself in any such relationship before this period: another instance of Nasreen's ageing impact on me.) Thomas Wentworth Higginson, the well-meaning minor-league *littérateur* approached for guidance by Emily Dickinson, must have been somewhere in my mind, both as designated literary adviser ('Will you be my preceptor, Mr Higginson?' the poet famously wrote) and as the possible object of the erotic/mystic infatuation in Dickinson's unsent 'Master Letters': 'I want to see you more – Sir – than all I wish for in this world . . .'

But I'm overstating my feeling of avuncularity here. The truth is,

I saw us on a more equal footing than that: two writers, at different stages of our careers, but involved in similar struggles. And just as Nasreen felt free to interrogate me about my life and writing, so I felt free to ask her the kinds of questions I would have asked any other writer friend (or non-writer friend for that matter) who'd had first-hand experience of things that interested me.

To this end I asked two questions on subjects that were very much on my mind at that time. The first was a general one about what it was like for someone from the Muslim world to be in New York in the immediate aftermath of the 9/11 attacks. Nasreen answered this in the slightly manic style she sometimes adopted, full of high-speed lists and esoteric references – Razorfish, Dr Dave, Dharma Priestesses – none of it very illuminating. The second was about veils. Veils, burkas, yashmaks, niqabs and chadors had been a source of imagery for me since my first book of poems in 1987. Nasreen was clearly interested in the phenomenon of being a woman from an Islamic culture, and it seemed to me natural enough to ask her if she'd had any direct experience with veils. But it was a mistake.

'Would you like to see me in a veil, sir?' she wrote back. A deluge of fraught, breathless veil-related emails followed, indicating a belief (or at least a decision to believe) that my question was a sexual innuendo (evidently a welcome one) and culminating, on 11 October, in this: '. . . i spent nearly an hour in a lingerie shop contemplating veils today, James . . .'

By then I had exasperatedly told her to forget about veils, and with this last email I had to acknowledge that this correspondence of ours was becoming problematic. I didn't know what to do. I thought gloomily of the various college lawyers and deans of student affairs whose excruciating lectures to new faculty on how to conduct oneself with students so as to avoid a sexual harassment suit had been such a strange and surprising feature of my first years teaching in the States. (The paranoid extremes of self-monitoring that all this had prompted in me, along with the loathsome falsifications of consciousness it seemed to entail, had provided some of the content of my novel *The Horned Man*.) Not that Nasreen – mid-thirties, and two years out of graduate school – could exactly be considered my 'student', but even so, as I read this latest email I seemed to see those dismal figures wagging their fingers and murmuring *We warned you . . .*

I was in a jittery, distracted state during those weeks, brought on not by Nasreen but by a new development concerning our apartment. The owner of the management company that had recently bought our building had called up out of the blue to inform us that she'd found a note from the previous owner saying we lived upstate and that the apartment was no longer our primary residence. I'd made a blustering attempt to deny this, and the woman had countered, unexpectedly, by offering to buy us out of our lease. It wasn't a very large offer, and underneath it was a clear threat to start eviction proceedings if we didn't accept. But all the same it was a surprise to have money dangled in front of us like that: an unforeseen twist that complicated my unhappiness at possibly losing the apartment with a little sordid glitter of avarice. A lawyer told us we might be able to get substantially more than the owner was offering if we played our cards right, but also warned that if we held out for too much she might opt for settling the matter in Housing Court, in which case we would probably lose and end up with nothing. I'd begun to negotiate, very quickly finding myself in the grip of tumultuous feelings: greedy fantasies of an enormous payout, fear of being outmanoeuvred, anxiety over the loss of my lifeline to the city.

In the midst of all this, Nasreen's insistent, unstoppably amorous communications, often a dozen or more a day now, had begun to feel oppressive. I answered fewer and fewer of them, responding with just a line or two to those that I did. She noticed, of course, though if she was hurt (which of course she was), she had the grace to blame herself for overwhelming me, and limited her reproaches to the occasional semi-humorous aside ('why do you deny me???'), even as she kept up the barrage. On 21 October, in reply to a question about whether I was ill and if so whether this was why I hadn't written for so long, I said: 'No, but I can't keep up with all these emails you're sending.' This was my way of asking her to leave me alone for a while, but it had no effect on the torrent of emails, which continued unabated as the fall of 2006 drew to an end: a serial monologue about her love life, her Brooklyn apartment, various intrigues at work and the stress of finishing her novel.

In a casual way she often referred to herself as feeling 'crazy' or 'insane' or 'paranoid' about one thing or another. I didn't take this too seriously, but sometimes she did sound genuinely in pain and on one occasion I suggested she might want to get some professional help or advice. In reply she wrote: 'James, they are very silly, the things I say. I'm half joking when I freak out. I'm glad I'm convincing, however.' This added to the general irritated mood gathering in me – nobody likes being jerked around – and when a couple of similarly distressed emails arrived in November I didn't respond. And in fact I didn't write again until she demanded to know, once more, whether I was sick and I emailed back, tersely, to say that I wasn't.

There was an encouraging moment on 18 November, when she wrote:

> my work situation has made me nuts and you sort of
> became my lifeline during the day. I will stop and
> contact you when I finish the novel. Need to leave
> that job and you alone for a while.

The very reasonable tone of this seemed to suggest that my exasperation had finally got through to her, and that she understood. I was reassured, even felt cautiously confident that she would do as promised and that after a few weeks' silence we would go back to our old, pleasant, unfrenetic correspondence.

But the next day the torrent resumed.

That winter, as K—— and I started planning our trip to Provence, Nasreen's emails entered a distinct new phase of development.

In terms of subject matter, the main new theme was a situation that had arisen at her job. As I understood it, she was claiming to have had a brief affair with a colleague that had ended with each of them accusing the other of sexual harassment and the college terminating both of their contracts with three months' pay. In response, Nasreen had decided to launch a discrimination suit against the college, based on both gender and race. She hired a lawyer and began copying me (unasked) on her emails to him, sometimes with explanatory comments, sometimes not. In them the motifs of sex, gender, race, money and Middle Eastern politics mingle in strange ways. There is also a new tone, a sort of exhibitionistic boisterousness, that seemed to me as odd and out of character as the brashly melodramatic nature of the subject matter itself. 'This will be fun,' she enthuses to her lawyer. 'Let's call it legal performance art.' Again: 'I want to fight. I want this to be a circus . . .' She calls the suit 'a high-profile case, being that I'm Iranian . . . It involves sex, violence, and infringement of constitutional and employment rights . . . They've been treating me like a Guantanamo detainee . . .'

I didn't like being sent this stuff any more than I'd liked it when she forwarded me the email of her old classmate. I didn't like the careless flouting of basic codes of privacy. I didn't like the self-intoxicated tone. Above all I didn't like the galling sense of the discrepancy between the image I'd formed of Nasreen when I taught her – that gifted, reticent, subtly attractive person – and the character disclosing itself now. Had I misjudged her – projected some wishful image of my own making onto the enigmatic exterior she'd first presented (an image drawn, I suppose I must accept, from the corniest archetype of demure Middle Eastern womanhood as concocted in the Western male psyche)? If so, that made me a spectacularly lousy observer of human beings, a thought that in turn played directly into my insecurities concerning my aptitude for this profession of writer.

On the other hand, perhaps I hadn't misjudged her. Perhaps she was simply changing, undergoing some kind of metamorphosis. In that case, was I implicated? Responsible? K——, who wasn't very interested in Nasreen or her emails, had nevertheless made a point of advising me not to break off contact with her, or not too abruptly. I'd sensed she was right, and throughout that winter I continued to think of my silence as a temporary suspension of communication – to be resumed as soon as Nasreen gave me breathing space – rather than a complete cut-off. But with every new email that arrived I felt more antagonised, less inclined to write back. And so the silence deepened.

As I experienced it, this silence of mine was a sort of self-cancelling argument between the impulse to respond and the growing sense of being imposed on. For Nasreen, however, I imagine (in retrospect) that the silence came across as something more controlled and monumental: the imperious silence of a man who no longer considers a woman worthy of his attention and has, as it were, pulled up the drawbridge.

This perception of me (if I am right about it) didn't affect the rate of her emails, but was perhaps a factor in their darkening mood. She starts claiming that bad things are happening to her. The colleague accusing her of harassment at work has broken into her computer. Her boss is somehow conniving with him. Parts of her novel have been erased. I didn't believe any of this and I didn't really believe she believed it either. I suspected her of simulating a state of nervous anxiety in order to get me to react, and the strong sense that she was trying to manipulate me made me even less inclined to write back.

Pleas, reproaches, bits of ruefully lucid self-analysis, little lightning flickers of anger alternate in rapid succession as 2006 draws to an end. The harried feeling of being at the receiving end of increasingly unwanted attention still vied with some vague sense that I ought to respond in some way, and at this point I was still imagining that I would, as soon as there was enough space between one email and the next to get over my annoyance and generally overwhelmed feeling, but there never was, and moreover the content of them was increasingly of a nature that made me wary. 'you love me james. i know you're busy but this is more fun. tell me to stop and write my novel' . . . 'your silence is scary, sir, but probably necessary' . . . 'have fun in Provence. brother saw an article on you in Chronicle and i google-stalked you . . . again.'

As the new year began, preparations for our trip to France became more concerted. The logistics of pulling our two kids from school for four months, finding someone to look after our house, and setting up places to stay in all the regions we were proposing to cover for our book were complicated and time-consuming. Negotiations over our apartment were still grinding on, though it was becoming clear that we weren't going to make the killing I'd fantasised, which, if nothing else, streamlined my feelings on that subject into more or less uncomplicated depression.

And all the while, present under each day like the murmur of some underground river, was the steady flow of Nasreen's emails into my inbox. I didn't answer them. I couldn't think of anything to say that wouldn't either encourage further deluges or else sound too bluntly unfriendly. Still, it bothers me, this silence of mine. I can remember all the reasons for it. I can easily recall the feeling of being oppressed and disillusioned and even in some way taken advantage of. I can summon back exactly the sense of having not so much broken off contact as suspended it until things, as I vaguely put it to myself, 'got back to normal'. I can state very confidently, knowing what I know now about Nasreen, that even if I hadn't stopped responding when I did, I would have been forced to sooner or later and events would have unfolded in the same disastrous way as they did. And yet I can't help feeling there was something hard about it; that if I were a person in a novel, it would show as a significant character flaw, a failure of empathy.

At the end of February 2007, I flew with my family to Marseilles.

There is the fortress fantasy, to which I am certainly prone, but there is also the fantasy of motion, of being the knight errant ('Sir James') who ventures forth on a quest, a journey, a mission, and this, at some level, was why we were in France.

I'm not sure if it counts as the full chivalric 'venture' if you ride out accompanied by the entire population of your fortress; i.e. your family. It may be that all I had done was to set my fortress on wheels and roll it through the French countryside. But I was certainly occupied, physically and mentally, to the absolute limit of my capacity, and that, for the moment, appeared to be enough to satisfy this particular fantasy.

We were on the move almost constantly, driving around to get the lie of the land, then walking – ten, twelve, fifteen miles a day – in search of itineraries that met the very specific requirements of our book: unspoiled landscapes, navigable trails, good places to eat along the way. In between, we were poring over maps and old French hiking guides, while also trying to keep our children on top of their schoolwork. And every couple of weeks we moved house to another part of the enormous region, packing up and heading off into the unknown.

An unexpected bonus of this nomadic life was how little opportunity there was to sit in front of a computer screen. None of the *gîtes* we rented had Internet connections, so we had to wait to get our email till we found ourselves near a library or Internet cafe. This happened only rarely, and we were always in a hurry when it did. Without fail there would be twenty or thirty emails from Nasreen in my inbox. I didn't answer any of them. Most I deleted without reading. Those I did read continued along the same lines as before: updates on this absurd-sounding lawsuit of hers, descriptions of her new job at a wine store, complaints about her landlord in Brooklyn. Innocuous stuff, except, again, for the sheer quantity of it, and for the habit of forwarding her correspondence with other people.

Concerning the latter, there was one possibly significant new development. She had placed an ad in the personal column of the *London Review of Books* (I had once told her a story about a friend of mine who did this – a jokey story, but I assume it was what gave her the idea), and among the emails she had now begun forwarding me was the intimate correspondence resulting from this ad. She had met, among other lonely hearts, an English academic who had left his wife and daughter after having an affair, and the two of them were exchanging long emails that appeared to be largely about the current political situation: the Iraq war, the Blair/Bush alliance. I read a few of them, but in themselves they didn't seem all that remarkable (everyone, myself included, was obsessed with those subjects at that time), or not nearly as remarkable – or strange, or disturbing – as the fact that I was being forwarded them in the first place.

I tried to ignore this little undercurrent of weirdness as we made our way across Provence, but it wasn't easy. It was becoming clear to me that Nasreen wasn't going to conveniently fade away from my life just because I wanted her to (which by now I had to admit I did); that by some alchemy I didn't understand and certainly didn't want to believe I'd had any part in creating, I had become the object of an obsession.

We returned to the States in June 2007. The emails continued flooding in and I continued not answering them. The interesting writerly friendship I had thought I was embarking on had clearly been a figment of my imagination, and I felt mocked by my own naivety. I did have a vague sense of being under an obligation to read the novel if and when Nasreen finished it, but I was beginning to doubt she ever would. Meanwhile the deadline for our own book was September, which gave us less than three months to convert the mass of notes we'd accumulated into serviceable guidebook prose, and turn the piles of torn, creased, sweat- and rain-blotched maps we'd annotated and redrawn en route into presentable topographic diagrams. At the same time there were numerous minor re-entry crises to deal with – blown-over trees in the yard, damage done by a bear breaking into the house, groundhogs romping all over the vegetable garden.

All of which is to say that I was busy.

On 19 July Nasreen emailed a doubled photo of her face, cheek to cheek with itself, with the words: 'I should be committed . . .' A week later she sent another photo: bare-shouldered, mouth open, head tilted forward with hair hanging down either side, curtaining off one eye, the other staring out with a dazed look. 'i'm really scared and very blocked!'

I didn't know what to make of these, but I felt, obscurely, that I was being warned that if I didn't respond, some kind of craziness would ensue.

The next day a long email arrived: '**the novel and where it stands**', ran the heading.

```
James, if you care, even, I've written a little status
report . . . I'm still unsure why you dislike me so.
I rather liked being your little pup.
```

Aggrieved tone aside, it was a sober and fairly coherent account of what she had been trying to do with her novel. If those photos with their odd captions had been oblique threats of craziness, this was perhaps the obverse, a sample of the return to sanity I could expect if I chose to respond. I didn't like the carrot any more than the stick, but for all my strong desire – stronger than ever – not to be back in touch with her, I didn't see how I could refuse to read the revisions she'd made to her novel, since I was so implicated, by now, in the book's existence. She wasn't actually asking me to read anything yet (and it wasn't clear that she had anything new to read), but I sensed that she wanted me to offer, or at least to show myself willing to take an interest, and I was resigned to doing so.

That evening, as I was mulling over what to say to her, an email arrived, headed '**a coward would not read this**'. The text continued:

```
and you're probably not reading it or you are because you
are hoping to cull some material. well, fuck you . . .
you're unethical, an "irresponsible hippy." And stop
all your rationalizing about feeding the family and all
that bullshit.
    You had no integrity with me and you're using a God
given talent to say nothing. And I don't want to hear
about your family because your kids have a future of
being thought of as Nazi Germans.
```

This was the first directly and unequivocally hostile email she'd sent. Later that evening came another:

```
when I needed help you disappeared. And wrote a
fucking story in which I am obviously the psychopathic
jaywalker.
```

I'll come back to this 'jaywalker' story later, along with the re-mark in the earlier email about my alleged desire to 'cull' her emails for 'material', a theme that was to develop significantly over the next few weeks. But in the meantime, just to stay with the events of what turned out to be a momentous evening, twenty minutes later another email arrived that introduced what was perhaps the most discon-certing of the half-dozen-odd new themes ushered in during the tumultuous onset of this new phase. Was I disappointed, Nasreen asks, that she had

```
yelled and screamed a little about how fucking crazy Jews
are these days? It's fucking TRUE. Stupid and crazy.
I can't say that but hundreds of thousands of Arabs can
die in silence? I don't fucking think so, sir . . .
SIR
```

Aside from anything else, this was just plain puzzling to me. She had never, as far as I remembered, said anything about Jews before, let alone 'yelled and screamed' about them, and I'd never raised the subject myself. I'd published, long before I met her, a book of poems that explored some of the convolutions of my own Anglo-Jewish background, as well as an article about my father that further aired the subject, and Nasreen had – as later became apparent – read both, but in both it is manifestly clear, or I thought it was, that I am not a supporter of Israel's military policy, let alone any kind of Zionist, so it was very strange to find myself cast suddenly as some kind of would-be silencer of Arabs. Still, this was a relatively benign, even tentative, sounding of the new motif: a test, perhaps, to see how she *herself* was going to feel about elevating the terms of her grievance against me into something more grand and global.

Judging from the first email to arrive the next morning, she felt all right about it:

```
I think the holocaust was fucking funny and about as
hilarious as the holocaust industry . . .
   How about that, SIR?
```

The same email introduces another new theme, also to become a
major element in the sustained tirade that had just begun. This was
my apparent misconduct as a teacher, in which capacity I was now
accused of having deliberately humiliated her:

```
You're so self-serving, you were willing to try to make
the stupid class made up of a bunch of shitty American
low-lives laugh at my expense after Thanksgiving break.
   "Oh, and how was your thanksgiving, Nasreen?"
```

I had no idea what this referred to, but anyway had no time to
think about it: a few minutes later another email arrived, bringing
another major new theme into play: my apartment, though as yet it
was unclear what her precise target was here. '**Morgan College, your
brothel**', runs the heading:

```
that's what it is. that's why you have that apartment you
would not consider giving up to ACTUALLY HELP SOMEONE.
```

A little later she returns to the theme of my exploiting her life in
my work, spiking it with the following (presumably) sarcastic suggestion, and thereby introducing yet another theme into the great
fugue of hatred and malice that thundered over my life for the
next several years, namely the reprehensible nature of my writing in
general:

```
why don't you write some more exotic stories about
fucking your servants?
```

This, as she confirmed in the next, more public phase of her attack, refers to a short story of mine, 'The Siege', about a relationship between an Englishman and a married woman from an unnamed Third World country who lives in his basement and cleans his house in lieu of rent. Half an hour later my novel *The Horned Man* comes in for similar treatment:

> what is the bottom line of horned man? that men should
> fuck everything in sight so they don't become underground
> psycho killers?

Fresh attacks began the next morning. At one point she forwarded another round of correspondence with her English academic, with whom she was now also discussing my various wrongdoings:

> He took verbatim things I'd written him in an email and
> just tacked it onto his story. I'm sure my thoughts
> and ideas are all over his work by now . . . But he's
> a fraud and it'll all be exposed . . .

The intent here, among other things, seemed to be to convey to me that she was now planning to go public with her accusations, which indeed turned out to be the case, though not until those accusations had been substantially beefed up.

I was in a state of extreme bewilderment by now, my head reeling every time a new email arrived. K—— did her best to calm me down, telling me there was no point getting upset by something so obviously crazy. Her relaxed attitude to life has been a source of immeasurable comfort to me throughout our marriage in general and this saga in particular. But I've never quite learned to make it my own, and outside the immediate field of her practical good sense I would soon lapse back into my own more familiar, gnawing anxiety. At this point the anxiety was still closer to bafflement than to actual dread. Among other things, I simply couldn't connect the ferocity of Nasreen's words with the quiet, articulate student I had taught at Morgan College, or even with the annoyingly compulsive emailer she had become later. There was an untraversable chasm, it seemed to me, between this eruption of verbal violence and everything that had gone before. My silence, however poorly Nasreen understood it (but I think she understood it well enough – why else all those promises to leave me alone for a bit?), didn't seem enough to explain what had happened, but then what did? Had she really 'gone crazy', or was this all simply a desperate attempt to get me to react, a mask of madness put on to provoke a response? Possibly. At 9.36 that evening comes the cry:

```
You fucking faggot coward, say something!
```

She couldn't know it, of course, but I had been wanting very badly to 'say something' since the beginning of this onslaught, and in fact had typed out several emails to her, some enraged, some trying to strike a conciliatory note, some explaining at length all the reasons for my silence over the past few months. But in every case something had held me back from hitting the send button. Aside from my confusion about what to say, I was suddenly wary of what this forwarder of emails might do with anything I might send her.

I didn't know much, at that time, about the protocols of forging or altering emails from other people and resending them to recipients of your choice, or of determining the true identity of the sender (I have since become an expert), but instinctively, it seemed a mistake to deliver anything containing my own electronic DNA into Nasreen's possession. Though I didn't quite know it yet, I had entered the realm of stricken enchantment in which technology and psychology overlap, where the magical thinking of the primitive mind, with its susceptibility to spells, curses, witchcraft of every kind, converges with the paranoias peculiar to our own age.

```
9:45 p.m.:
Do you have to be the stereotype of a Jew, James?
```

A few seconds later:

```
I'm NOT in love with you, I want your apartment
```

```
9:48 p.m.:
give me your fucking keys.
```

By the next day, 2 August, I have become fully identified with Bush's America: '**your troops coming home** . . . ' runs the heading,

```
I hope they die, every single one of your money-making
gangster lowlives . . .
```

And a little later, in self-reflexive mode again, comes the comment:

```
I think this is called verbal terrorism.
```

I hadn't heard that phrase before. But as I came to appreciate Nasreen's grasp of the dynamics of assymetric conflict, where she had apparently nothing to lose, and I had everything, I realised that it was peculiarly apposite. I, as an Anglo-American Jew, a family man, a published author, a middle-aged male in a position of power (at least from her perspective), was the axis of, shall we say, 'virtue', while she, in her own mind at least, was the lone jihadi. It took a while for her to figure out the exact nature of her mission, but when it did finally clarify itself in her mind, she laid it out in her characteristically succinct and forceful way:

'I will ruin him.'

One hot morning, as K—— and I were on the porch of our barn, drawing maps, the phone rang. It was Janice Schwartz, my agent, and she sounded upset. For several days she had been receiving strange, unpleasant emails about me from Nasreen. She hadn't wanted to tell me at first, but now she herself was being attacked in the emails, and she was concerned for her safety. That morning a woman sounding very like Nasreen had called her. 'Can I speak to Meir Kahane?' the woman had asked, before hanging up. Meir Kahane was the ultra-Zionist rabbi whose follower Baruch Goldstein had massacred Muslims praying in the Cave of the Patriarchs in Hebron. Kahane himself was assassinated in 1990, shot in the neck.

Janice forwarded me the emails. The first, dated 1 August, strikes a businesslike tone:

Janice,
I'm sure James is not reading my emails anymore, so
I'd appreciate it if you'd tell him that I didn't
appreciate him using my words and ideas I'd expressed
in emails verbatim in the short story about the psychotic
jaywalker.

The next is less controlled:

. . . after reading that short story in which my private
words to him jumped at me (and I'm not talking about
silly stock-character shit like her drug use, but.

39

```
rather, her feelings on surrender and vulnerability), I'm
left to think that he was being parasitic. Seductively
parasitic.
    And I'm pissed. And I wanted to share it with you. Why
not? You're not interested in my work and you support
your little boy and all he can do to bring you both
money.
    So, as you can see, reading the psychotic jaywalker
story has made me very angry.
```

'**His future stories . . .**' runs the heading of the next:

```
Better not be things he stole from me. Listen, lady I'm a
real person who's spent her whole life trying to survive
because I live in a fucked up sadistic country . . .
    . . . if your little boy, who you're so impressed with
for aping a white Englishman, steals anything else from
me and I have to see it in print when I deserved to be
given a level playing field to write my novel, not pumped
for his amusement, there will be hell to pay.
    I'm livid—and rightfully so
    I was not put on earth to feed James Lasdun's
children. I hope you can understand that.
```

Later that day Nasreen sets her sights on Paula Kurwen, the
editor to whom Janice had introduced her. For the moment Paula's
offence is merely that she 'was an elegant middle-class post-Nazi
era Jewess living in America. In other words, she was privileged.'
Nevertheless, she, too, is implicated: 'You all play a part in un-
leashing the fury.'

A minute or so later, with this 'fury' now apparently reaching for
terms strong enough to account for its own escalating intensity,

Nasreen brings on one of those words that scorch everything they come near. The word is 'rape'. It isn't the first time she has used it, but it is the first time she has used it in connection with me and, even though she uses it figuratively rather than literally, I feel immediately the disfiguring potency of its touch, as if I have been splashed with acid:

> I say if I can't write my book and get emotionally and
> verbally raped by James Lasdun, a Jew disguising himself
> as an English-American, well then, the Holocaust Industry
> Books should all be banned as should the films.

It is one thing to be abused in private: you experience it almost as an internal event, not so different from listening to the more punitive voices in your own head. But to have other people, people you know and care about, brought into the drama, whether as witnesses or collateral victims or both, is another matter. It confers a different order of reality on the abuse: fuller and more objective. This strange, awful thing really is happening to you, and people are witnessing it.

Along with the accusations of theft, Janice had also received details of my supposed (but entirely fictitious) affair with Nasreen's former classmate Elaine, complete with descriptions of various kinky sexual practices that Nasreen claimed to have heard I went in for (she had an uncanny way with that transparent and yet curiously effective device of rumour, the unattributed source: 'I'm told he . . .' 'I hear he . . .' 'Everyone knows he . . .').

Regardless of whether Janice believed a word of these emails (and she assured me she didn't), my impulse was to deny them indignantly. But even as I was forming the words I felt the futility of doing so. Intrinsic to the very nature of Nasreen's denunciations and insinuations was, as I began to understand, an iron law whereby the more I denied them, the more substance they would acquire, and the more plausible they would begin to seem. Their very wildness was a part of their peculiar power. On the basis of there being no smoke without fire (so I imagined Janice, and then Paula, and then, as things got worse, all sorts of other people, thinking), surely something as black and billowing as these emails must indicate that I was guilty of *something*, and that even if I wasn't unscrupulous or weird or fucked up in the precise way Nasreen claimed, I probably was in some other, related way. For the first time in my life I began to consider the word 'honour' as something more than an antique formula, and the word 'reputation' as something other than an index of value in the literary marketplace.

But the 'psychotic jaywalker'.

Something bizarre happened to me when I first arrived in New York, in 1986. I was walking down a quiet street in the West Village when I heard a woman's voice calling 'Sir, sir, excuse me, sir' from a window at the top of a narrow town house. The door to her apartment was stuck, she said, and she was trapped inside. Would I come up and help her get it open? She sounded pleasant enough, laughing a little at her own helplessness, but I'd heard too many horror stories about New York not to be suspicious, and my instinct was to keep moving. Still, I hesitated, and a moment later I was gloomily climbing the dark stairway to her floor, certain I was being set up to be mugged.

Outside her apartment I tried opening the door with the handle, but I couldn't get it to engage with the opening mechanism. I pushed the door, but that didn't work either. 'Try taking a run at it,' the woman called from the other side. The imagined mugging gave way, in my mind, to something worse: I was going to be framed for breaking and entering or whatever they called it here, blackmailed, sent home in disgrace . . . Resigning myself, I went to the end of the narrow hallway and ran full tilt at the door, hurling myself against it as hard as I could. It flew open, revealing a cluttered, brick-walled studio, with a bed in the corner and the woman – dark-haired, well dressed, attractive – looking at me, startled. She thanked me profusely. There was no mugger, no blackmail camera, nothing untoward at all.

But as I stood in the doorway, the situation seemed to take on a new, unexpected complexion, in which I myself was the source of menace. I was a man who had just broken open the door to a strange woman's apartment, and this large fact somehow overshadowed, even seemed to obliterate, the perfectly innocent explanation behind it. The woman appeared suddenly nervous. She did ask if she could offer me a cup of coffee, but I felt she was doing so only out of politeness and that to accept, even just to linger there talking to her (both of which I found myself wanting to do), would have been to take advantage of the situation in an underhand way. I declined politely and left, reflecting on how the desire to appear scrupulously honourable (itself based entirely on the fact that I had found her attractive and wanted her to find *me* attractive) had required me to do precisely the thing that would guarantee no further contact between us.

There was something else too that lingered with me: an atmospheric quality that, like the equivocal mood of certain dreams, continually drew my mind towards it but then, every time I came close to identifying what it was, seemed to evaporate.

For months I tried to write a story about the episode, but I couldn't figure out how to make it work as fiction. Twenty years later, however, just before I set off for Provence with my family, I found myself thinking of it again and a new approach occurred to me.

This consisted of telling the story in two parts: one from the man's point of view, the other from the woman's. The first part kept close to the facts as I recalled them. The second was of course purely speculative, and reflected a change in the way I had come to think about the woman herself, a change based on that dim sense I'd had of some mysterious further dimension to the encounter, which I had never satisfactorily accounted for. Unlike the simple, practical-minded damsel in distress I had made of her at the time (a projection, I suppose, of my own relative naivety – I was twenty-eight), she is now a complicated figure: isolated, a bit reckless and full of strong desires of her own. Her door has jammed once in the past, we discover. She called to a man for help and after he forced it open, the two of them, jarred out of their usual selves, ended up in her bed. Since then, she has taken to jamming the door deliberately when she feels like company, and watching at the window for men to lure up (though 'lure' suggests something sinister, whereas all she wants is the warmth and connection of freely reciprocated desire). The Englishman she beckons up on the day the story takes place turns out to be younger and more innocent-looking than she had judged from his appearance on the street below her, and this unsettles her. His polite reserve makes her even more nervous, but she perseveres, offering him the usual cup of coffee. His refusal, followed by his abrupt disappearance, upsets her badly – this hasn't happened before. Still, with the help of a stiff drink she recovers, and soon, having reset the catch in the door, she is back at her window, fondly remembering past encounters while gazing down at the street in preparation for the next.

There are no drugs in the story (only a glass of vodka), and no jaywalkers, psychotic or otherwise, but this is the story Nasreen refers to as my 'psychotic jaywalker' story. I wrote it quickly and sent it off before we flew to Marseilles. It was published in a British magazine while we were in Provence, and at some point was put in the magazine's online archive, where Nasreen found it, presumably while 'google-stalking' me.

In her many accusations of theft concerning this story, she never spelled out exactly what it was I was supposed to have stolen. But she did copy me on emails that she had begun sending out to other people (the public-defamation aspect of her campaign was widening now, and she wanted me to know about it) in which my various misdeeds are recounted, among them this alleged plagiarism. Even in these emails the details are a bit hazy, but they centre on the idea of surrender. The clearest statement of them comes in an email she copied me on, to a former classmate – I'll call her Sandy – in which Nasreen writes:

```
well, the piece James wrote and why it bothered me was
there was a section and in that section he wrote, nearly
verbatim, what i'd said to him—my ideas on surrender (I
was linking sado-masochism with the image of the lady of
justice, balancing scales . . .)
     . . . this was my conversation about it and surrender
(islam means surrender) . . . and not only did he co-opt
it, he made the character out to be a psychotic
jaywalker . . .
```

It is possible that Nasreen did send me an email talking about such things, and that it was among the many from that early, friendly phase that I didn't keep. It's also possible that her words resembled the passage she seems to be referring to in my story, where the woman reflects on her discovery of the inverse power of surrender. The passage in my story begins: 'There were ways in which the world forced itself on you and you had no choice but to yield. But there were also ways of using your own weakness as a source of strength.'

A description of how the woman discovered this paradoxical strength follows, along with details of times in her past when she has used it, and then the passage concludes: 'It wasn't about willpower; it was about submission. That was the glory of it.'

Early on in this steadily deepening crisis, I began to find myself drifting occasionally into a courtroom fantasy in which I was defending myself against Nasreen's various charges. On the subject of this alleged theft, I would picture myself taking the stand with a calm expression that nevertheless contained a glint of clenched anger. Strutting before me, thumbs hooked in his waistcoat as he grins and winks at the jury, Nasreen's attorney reads out the passage I have quoted above and asks if the words and thoughts are entirely my own.

Yes, I reply.

He asks if I recall an email from Nasreen in which she discusses similar ideas about the secret power inherent in the gesture of surrender or, as I put it, '*submission*' (and he assumes a snide expression here, as if to imply that nobody is fooled by my substitution of a synonym for his client's word).

I do not, I tell him.

With a sly grin he produces an email, dated sometime in 2006, and reads aloud a few sentences in which Nasreen does, indeed, appear to be articulating a similar idea. The jury members look at me askance.

Well, sir, the attorney says, I suppose you will now attempt to persuade the court that the resemblance, the remarkably *close* resemblance if I may say so, between these two passages is purely coincidental?

No, I say, it isn't coincidental at all.

The attorney looks startled, though he contrives to give his shock a deliberately staged appearance.

Oh?

Both passages are borrowed, I tell him. From the same source.

Indeed?

He rolls his eyes a little in the direction of the jury: this fellow before us appears to be not only a scoundrel and a fraud but also the village idiot, and we must now prepare ourselves to be greatly amused.

46

Leaving aside your earlier statement, he continues, that these thoughts were entirely your own, and passing over the question of whether you have therefore just admitted to perjuring yourself, perhaps you would be good enough to tell us what this common *source* might be?

Certainly.

Reaching into my briefcase, I produce a battered paperback, and hand out photocopies of a page from the book's introductory essay, drawing the jury's attention to the following passage, concerning the importance of the gesture of renunciation to the author under discussion:

The closer you look at him, the more central the gesture seems, both to his life and his writing, and the more it appears to invert itself into a paradoxical tool for its opposite, taking possession.

The attorney frowns, pantomiming irritated bewilderment as to the relevance of this, but I read on, quoting another passage, highlighted in fluorescent yellow marker for the jury's benefit, that describes how the act of renunciation becomes:

a means of leveraging one's very powerlessness so as to exert power . . .

Darting a glance at the jury, the attorney gives his copy of the pages a dismissive shake.

Even suppose we accept some similarity in the general sentiments here, he says, why should we accept that this essay rather than my client's email was the source of your words?

Because I *wrote* it, I tell him, icily.

I let the jury examine the book, a New York Review of Books

edition of Italo Svevo's novel *As a Man Grows Older*. On its cover are the words 'Introduction by James Lasdun'. In the front matter is the publication date, 2001.

While they absorb the implications of this, I reach into my briefcase for more books and photocopies. Here is the Penguin Classics edition of D. H. Lawrence's *St Mawr*, published in 2006, with my introduction, from which I read my analysis of the heroine's journey as yet another instance of the power of letting go:

> Lou's grand processional journey from London to New Mexico takes her through a series of shatterings and disavowals: friendship, love, marriage, England, St Mawr himself . . . These function as the principle of growth in her psyche: she becomes steadily more capacious as a character with everything she relinquishes.

Here is a volume of my poetry from 1997 with a poem about a man who gives away all his possessions:

> . . . each object's
> Hollowed-out void successively
> More vivid in him than the thing itself,
> As if renouncing merely gave
> Density to having . . .

After passing out a few more samples further illustrating the point, I rest my case. And from the sympathetic looks directed at me from the jury, it seems to me I have proved not only that the ideas about surrender in my 'psychotic jaywalker' story are not taken from Nasreen, but also that any ideas Nasreen may have believed she herself had on that subject are most likely (avid reader of my work as her emails show her to be) taken from *me*.

It's a consoling fantasy, and it serves the function it evolved to fulfil: of enabling me to exonerate myself, over and over, in the arena of public opinion, which (as I imagined it in my increasingly harried state) was a vast space full of people with nothing better to do than examine me and watch me suffer.

But there is a private question that lingers:

Why, after being unable to write that story for twenty years, was I suddenly able to write it when I did?

Was it because I finally had a character – Nasreen's – on whom to model the woman in the story, and thereby bring it to life? If so, what does that say about my perception of Nasreen, and what does this perception say about my interest in her?

I hadn't been conscious of modelling the woman on her. There is no particular physical resemblance between them, no suggestion of anything Middle Eastern about the woman's background, which, to the small extent that I describe it, is thoroughly American.

Her behaviour, however, is another matter. For one thing, it now seems to me completely implausible. What real woman would do this: fake a broken door to lure men up to her apartment in the hope of a spontaneous fuck? I had been reading Maupassant's stories around the time of writing, and I think I imagined this action of hers would come over as something like the hard-edged erotic avidity you find in his studies of Parisian men and women, with something amusingly worldly and raffish about it. But it doesn't come over as anything like that. It comes over as the action of a woman who is either seriously disturbed, or else very obviously just a cipher in a fantasy of the writer who dreamed her up.

The notion of an attractive woman offering herself with no strings attached and no need for the effort or skills of seduction (no need, in fact, for any preliminaries at all) is, I imagine, a fairly standard component of male fantasy. It certainly is in mine. A voice calls to you from on high, from out of the blue, like some supernatural being who has read your mind, heard your prayer, the mumble of your everlasting need, which may be narrowly sexual or may have more to do with jolting yourself out of the settled patterns of your life, however pleasant that life might be, and all you have to do is acquiesce, surrender, and there you are, face-to-face with her, beside her bed . . .

It seems to me possible that I was motivated to write this story at least partly by the idea of imagining such a being, and that I was able to do this, finally, by combining my memory of the original woman with certain resonances from my first impressions of Nasreen, Nasreen's first emails having come at me out of the blue (or at least out of a two-year silence) like the voice of the woman in the window, calling for help like her, and curiously similar to her in their amusedly courteous tone and language: *Sir, sir, excuse me, sir . . .*

The fact that the young Englishman in my story is resistant to her charms, gallantly rescuing her from her ostensible plight while failing to acknowledge the underlying emotional plea, if anything further cements the connection, offering, as it does, an accurate representation both of my own irreproachably 'correct' behaviour with Nasreen and of the extent to which this depended on ignoring more complicated elements in the picture. He remains unaware of her designs on him, as he does of any desires of his own that might have led him up to her apartment in the first place. But both are known, of course, to his author, fabricator of this impeccably English mask, and of the fantastical femme fatale herself, who sends her curses after him as he vanishes out of her life: 'Goddam Englishman . . . ' just as Nasreen was to do when I vanished out of her life a few months later.

So I stand guilty of appropriating some kind of echo or semblance of Nasreen's 'essence', for literary purposes. Not a crime, perhaps, in the eyes of the ordinary world, but by my own standards definitely troubling, if only for its very strange consequence: that the hybridisation seems to have doubled back from the purely fictional realm into the realm of reality, with Nasreen exhibiting symptoms of a disturbance as deep as that of the woman in my story, and doing so more vividly the more closely she identified with her. As she herself was to write a few months later: 'i'm living your short story out and I'm scared.' This troubles and perplexes me quite a bit. It is as if in writing a character to some extent modelled on her, I am also guilty of modelling *her*, in turn, on the character: of causing her to develop her own version of the 'psychotic' behaviour of the woman at the window.

We are in the realm of the Gothic here: mind control, telepathic metamorphosis, whatever you want to call it. I don't believe in such things; I'm embarrassed even to mention them, and I wouldn't, were it not for the fact that this peculiar mechanism of reciprocity was to become a steadily more pronounced feature of the story as things got worse, and that, moreover, it began to work as much on me, after a while, as on Nasreen. So much so that, by a certain point, we were both, in effect, creating or re-creating each other in the image of our crassest fear, our most cravenly stereotyping fantasy: the Demon Woman, shall we say, and the Eternal Jew.

Good Morning
You pose as an intellectual but you're a corrupt thief.

Do you have to be the stereotype of a Jew, James? Oh, I see all the white male writers are doing it too . . .

I want your apartment because you owe it to me because you were miserable and you sucked my nectar and didn't help me when you should have . . .

what is wrong with your people?

do any of you have any ideas of your own? after you kill
all of "us" what will you do? everything you have is
stolen . . . there will be nothing left to steal!

Subj: Fwd: Re: (more notes on your sadistic world)
To: [Sandy]
. . . I was begging for help. And fine, who the fuck am I?
A former student, someone he could get a little "lift"
from in the midst of his mid-life . . . Fine, but it
hurts to see that he thinks me worthy of something to
steal but not to support in any real way for it to
be my own.

Subj: why do I bother forwarding this shit?
To: [her English academic]
James. He's an innocent bystander. It's almost as if he
just walked past a window and I manipulatively called
down for help. "Sir . . . Sir?"

Look, muslims are not like their Jewish counterparts, who
quietly got gassed and then cashed in on it . . . my
people are crazy motherfuckers and there will be hell to
pay for what your people have done to them . . .

Subj: signs of the end of the world . . .
began with Janice's limping.
    why the fuck did you send me to her? was this supposed
to be a joke on me? an inside jew-joke?
    ha ha ha ha! So nice of you. And I'm a psychotic
jaywalker because I believe in God and haven't sold my
soul to American cash?

you couldn't have, without all the bullshit
(incestuously paid-for) rave reviews you get, found
me an agent to work with?
[. . .]
You steal.
You steal.
You steal.
Call it antisemitism, I call what you do arrogance and
I call it disgusting.

Subj: I want my money back . . .
For the term you "taught me" and for the term you were
my "advisor" but couldn't even remember to bring me
my work.

Subj: apologies . . .
I hope you don't take anything I say seriously. I
understand everyone is too chickenshit to help an insane
woman. And no, I don't expect you to pay me for what
you stole. it happens all the time and why should you
care about my nervous breakdowns? I never even fucked
you . . .

Subj: a real, unpsychotic note
[. . .]
You are a kind man, James. I don't think you're the
caricature of a white man but I'm hoping I've pissed you
off. It brings color to the cheeks.

Mr. Horned God.
So tacky!

Subj: surrender . . .
you must be so perplexed.

   i'm hoping my mean-streak doesn't lend itself
to calling your management company and telling
them you rent the apartment out on weekends. I
would. I hope I don't. I really firmly believe that
you need to absolve your guilt by giving me your
keys.

   [. . .]

   (I hope I'm scaring you slightly. That would be
exciting.)

— — — — —

I also believe you are on medication instead of dealing
with why you and most Jewish people are sadistic. That is
why your writing falls flat.

— — — — —

Subj: Harriet too . . . you fucked her too?
Is that right?

   Well, I almost feel sorry for her because she
obviously went from being a good writer to turning in
nothing and you stole her writing too . . . in that
story. You stole from everyone in our class.

   [. . .]

   I don't feel that bad for her. She was another
vicious, overly competitive Jewess . . .

— — — — —

I wish ill health and disaster . . .
for you and your family.
Baruch adonai,
Nasreen

— — — — —

```
jews in america
need to shut up. the crazy shit that comes out of your
mouths spreads far and wide in a city filled with blacks,
muslims and asians who've had it: This sort of projection
doesn't work and all of you pussies who sit around
writing stupid shit and stealing from little girls are
just as much to blame.
      [ . . . ]
   Go forward this to the anti-defamation league. They're
criminals too . . .
```

So the summer continued.

I was bewildered, stunned, appalled, but at this time I didn't take the actual content of the emails very deeply to heart. I regarded the outburst as something entirely freakish: an eruption of irrational fury that, unpleasant as it was to witness, had nothing to do with me personally. It would end soon, I believed, either in silence or in a mortified apology (a genuine one that would unconditionally retract all the false accusations instead of reserving the right, as her occasional 'conciliatory' emails always did, to continue calling me a thief if I failed to respond).

Sometime in the fall, Nasreen announced that she was going to move to California, where her family lived. The decision seemed to soften her tone. She appeared (though it's hard to be certain) to be making fun of herself:

```
. . . I need to leave the East Coast where everyone
is racist and crazy. Besides, I am unsafe here
and the annoying trustfund hipsters raise my blood
pressure.
```

```
Love,
Nasreen, the peace-seeking and relentless verbal
terrorist.
```

There was even what appeared to be the beginnings of an explanation for her behaviour:

```
I really hope you and Paula and Janice understand my
bitter comments. I know you know what it's like to be in
character. I always have a hard time snapping out . . .
```

Being 'in character', presumably for her novel, wasn't a very convincing explanation for her emails (there were no anti-Semites in her novel), but the fact that she seemed to think they needed to *be* explained seemed encouraging. It was December by now, and with the year winding down and Nasreen moving to the other side of the country, I was cautiously hopeful that the whole unpleasant episode might be coming to an end.

But my optimism was misplaced.

Over the previous year there had been a spate of novels and memoirs, some of them best-sellers, published by youngish women of Iranian origin. Many of these books, I gathered (I hadn't read any of them), dealt with the period of the Shah's downfall and the rise of the fundamentalists, which was the period Nasreen had been attempting to cover in her own novel.

Even the most well-balanced writers are prone to anxiety about their work being pre-empted by other books. I suffer from it myself. So it wasn't a huge surprise to learn that Nasreen was unhappy about these rival publications. What *was* surprising, though perhaps it shouldn't have been, was to find out how she intended to deal with this unhappiness.

'You and Paula pandered my work' was the first clear indication.

Over the next few weeks, murkily, but with steadily growing conviction, Nasreen began to elaborate a theory in which I and various Jewish cohorts were guilty of deliberately preventing her from finishing her book so that we could steal her ideas and sell them to these other writers, most of whom happened to be Jewish as well as Iranian.

Like all conspiracy theories, this required constant adjustment in order to accommodate both Nasreen's own shifting grievances and the obstinate bits of reality that stood in its way. Sometimes I appear to be acting alone; sometimes the complexity of the charges requires me to have been in league with one or both of my 'yentas' (Janice and Paula), and sometimes the scale of my operation is perceived to be so vast that Nasreen is forced to link me to entirely new networks of co-conspirators, including, at one time, most of the faculty of the Morgan College writing programme. So too with the authors we're accused of helping: sometimes the denunciations focus on one in particular, sometimes two or more are grouped together, and there are periods in which I and my gang appear to be supplying as many as four desperate, unscrupulous writers with Nasreen's material, all at the same time.

A kind of feedback effect occurs now, between the increasingly villainous scenarios Nasreen imagines and the pitch of her rage, each intensifying the other. 'Janice gives you manuscripts . . .' begins one,

```
that you type up in your boring trying-to-be-white style.
you are the downfall of a culture. go back to england. we
don't want you here.
    [ . . . ]
    We rule now, your ways are OVER: you're all dying
off . . .
        get a toupe.
```

The emails become more apocalyptic in tone:

```
oh what will happen to you all . . . your stupid
fortress . . . your stupid stupid life made from other
people's blood and sweat . . .
```

More overtly threatening:

```
X [one of the Iranian authors] is fucked. And if you have
something to do with this, you are too . . .
```

More bitterly sarcastic:

```
i hope the money is worth it
when should i expect to see the rest of my work stolen?
```

More firmly accusatory even in their moments of apparent lucidity:

```
I'm sorry I fell in love with you but I don't understand
why you're punishing me with the books that have come out
```

More wide-ranging in their vitriol, as in this group email addressed to me, Paula, and Y (another Iranian writer, somehow involved in our conspiracy):

```
Y, keep your cunts-on-a-leash away from my material.
[ . . . ] You're all pathetic, and I've had enough of your
thievery. If you don't have a single thought of your own
and your little empty-headed heiresses don't either, spare
the American reader. But do not touch my work. I know what
you're all up to and so do writers much more influential
than anyone in your circle of crows.
```

More menacing in their demands for compensation:

```
I want every cent . . .
of what James made in "ghostwriting" from my emails for 7
[another 'buyer'] the whore. Or else I'm going to make him
pay in other ways.
```

And more fantastically comprehensive in the evils they attribute to me:

```
Boycott this man, for God's sake. He's the reason behind
terrorism.
```

By now, early 2008, I was beginning to feel seriously harassed, though it was still the tone of the emails rather than the content that was getting to me: the violent hatred they projected, rather than the accusations themselves. These latest ones, in particular, seemed too self-evidently preposterous to worry about. I was even a little relieved that they were as wild as they were. Who could possibly take seriously this idea that I was some kind of literary racketeer who had stolen her material in order to sell it off to other writers? It was too ridiculous to pay any attention to. I also felt, despite the widening embarrassment it entailed, protected by the growing number of people Nasreen now appeared to have in her sights. By this time she had copied me on emails she'd sent not only to Janice and Paula but also to several other writers and teachers she considered part of my conspiracy. These emails reserve their worst venom for me, but since they also attacked the recipients, they gave me a feeling of safety in numbers, at least on this particular front.

But I was forgetting the principles of assymetric warfare. I was forgetting my own observations about weakness as a source of strength, powerlessness leveraged into power. And I was forgetting the spirit of fair play that prevails among most people, whereby anyone claiming to have been victimised must be listened to with an open mind, however far-fetched the claim and however honourable-seeming the alleged victimisers.

'**James's Amazon Reviews, read em!**' runs the heading of the email Nasreen sent out on the morning of 30 December 2007. The email begins, in taunting parody of the tones of authentic victimhood: 'I hope I'm not in trouble for speaking the truth . . .'

I logged, very warily, on to Amazon.

The review, under the byline '**a former student of lasdun**', was posted on the page for my book *Seven Lies*. I'd never quite believed in the sensation you read about in novels of print swimming before a character's eyes at moments of high agitation, but that was precisely the effect. Words seemed to undulate as I looked at the screen. Phrases came in and out of focus: '. . . writers who teach at mfa programs like mr. lasdun . . .' '. . . my work was stolen . . .' '. . . after I told him I was raped while trying to finish my novel . . .' '. . . he used my writing (emails to him) in that story . . .'

Even with these preliminary reiterations of the familiar charges, I had the sensation that a new order of harm was being inflicted on me. First the private attacks had been extended to form that little intimate theatre of mortification comprised of my colleagues and acquaintances, and now a window had been opened up to the wider world. As if conscious of her new audience, Nasreen adopts a more measured voice. Laying aside the mask of naked rage, she poses instead as the scholar-victim who has taken it upon herself to deconstruct my work and expose the sociopathic attitudes encoded within it:

Having read Horned Man, I think he may have a penchant
for sadism. His short story "the Siege" is disturbing
in romanticising surveillance [. . .] It's also racist

in sexualizing a black woman from a "revolutionary"
country, who loves her husband but is demeaned and made
to have sex with "the english composer" to save her true
love's life.

You don't have to be a writer to imagine how it feels to find yourself the object of a malicious attack on the Internet. An ordinary
negative review is depressing, but it doesn't flood you with this sense
of personal emergency, as if not only your book but also your life, or
at least that large aura of meaning that accumulates around your life
and gives it value, is in imminent and dire peril. Call that aura your
'character', call it your 'good name', your 'reputation', your 'honour'.
Whatever it was, as I read the review on my screen I seemed to be
seeing, as if through a powerful medical instrument, the first stages
of some irreversible damage spreading into this nebulous yet indispensable entity. However crudely Nasreen may have been deploying
the gestures of critical theory and gender studies in her attempt to
brand me as a monster, it seemed to me that she had mounted a successful attack. Needless to say, her description of 'The Siege', like all
her other accounts of my work, bears little resemblance to the story
itself, but who was going to check? The semblance of an annihilating
critique had been created, and for people browsing the Web that is
all that matters. Here, for the casual shopper landing on my page,
was a reason to move on very quickly.

The multiplying effect of the Internet – the knowledge that anything on it can be infinitely reproduced – is a further element in the
alarm this kind of attack induces. So too is its odd nature as a mass
phenomenon in which, paradoxically, one participates in the blindest,
most solitary manner. Who else has seen what you have seen? Who
believes it? Who finds it entertaining? Who has copied it, posted it
elsewhere, emailed it to a friend? One never knows, but where malice
is involved, one quickly succumbs to the worst suspicions

But perhaps I was exaggerating the effect of this particular attempt at character assassination. Unless you are a celebrity, nobody is ever as interested in your reputation as you are. Certainly no one who saw the review would have paid it as much attention as I did. And given my modest readership, it's unlikely that many people ever *did* see it. As soon as I'd finished reading it I hit the 'report' button and fired off complaints to Amazon at every address I could find for them. I didn't get a reply, but after a few weeks the review was taken down. Similar reviews appeared on the Amazon pages of the authors I was accused of selling Nasreen's work to, and these too were taken down after a while. So I suppose I can't, after all, claim they did me serious harm.

But having raised the game to this freshly injurious level, Nasreen was hardly likely to give up exploring its possibilities. Her campaign, it appeared, was no longer aimed simply at expressing her anger, or at embarrassing me, but at something much more concrete and practical. It was at this time that she conceived that crystalline formulation of the true nature of her mission:

'I will ruin him.'

Part II

— — — — — — — —

Axes

But, having brought the story to this point, I must now commit the cardinal narrative sin of going backwards instead of plunging conventionally forwards. I do this because, inexplicable as Nasreen's actions ultimately seemed, I consider myself under an obligation to do everything in my power to account for them, and because I am aware that, in the interest of describing a complicated situation as quickly as possible, I have left things unsaid and failed to examine certain aspects of the situation as thoroughly as I should.

First of all, there is the question of the classroom.

I described Nasreen's reaction to my praise of her writing as 'unflustered', and so it appeared at the time. But of course it could not have been anything of the kind. When you have as much at stake as students do in these expensive, highly competitive programmes, you are not going to be 'unflustered' by your teacher's enthusiasm, however confident you may be in your abilities. I know this from my own experience. I studied English literature at university. There were no creative-writing classes on offer, but my tutor was a well-known poet and one day I plucked up the courage to hand him a sheaf of my poems. He was reluctant to take them, but a few weeks later I received a letter from him in which he praised them and encouraged me to go on writing. His words had a powerful, really almost a shattering, impact on me, one symptom of which was that for a very long time I was unable to relate to him as a normal human being. Having never been daunted by him before (or no more than any student is by their tutor), I suddenly found it hard to talk to him. I became nervous and awkward. Every exchange between us left me feeling anxious that I'd said something crass or offensive that would forfeit his good opinion. By giving me explicit authorisation to think of myself as a writer, he had become entangled in my fate, which in turn had imbued him – or, more precisely, caused my mind to flood its image of him – with godlike powers.

So I have to assume, or at least admit the possibility, that Nasreen had in fact been highly flustered by my admiration and that, as with my tutor, the experience had transformed me from a teacher respected merely out of convention into a figure of heightened power, similarly implicated in her fate; similarly crowned, robed and enthroned in her imagination. It's hard, almost impossible, for me to accept that such a version of myself, so unlike my own version of myself, could really exist in anybody's mind. But other than having to share the same physical appearance, there is no reason why other people's versions of oneself should bear a complete or even a remote resemblance to one's own. To repeat the words I myself quoted to Nasreen from George Eliot: 'The last thing we learn in life is our effect on other people.'

Next, there is the question of the 'fiancé'.

I had been struck by the word – the word itself – when she had used it, charmed by its old-fashioned aura, but I had given little thought to the drama of human embroilment it actually denoted. Even when the engagement ended, I had been more interested in her manner of disclosing the news ('I can't marry A—') – which had seemed to confirm my sense of her as someone who valued a certain reserve when it came to discussing personal matters – than in the news itself.

What I didn't consider, and no doubt should have even though I wasn't being invited to, was that she might have been traumatised by the break-up. As far as I understood, she had been the one to end it, but maybe she wasn't, and even if she was, she might well have been experiencing feelings of disappointment, failure, even the anguish of sexual jealousy that can afflict jilter and jilted alike in any break-up. People are always in various stages of various different dramas when you encounter them: freshly embarked on some, halfway or more through others. One is always approaching the denouement of this or that subplot of one's life. And you, the stranger, entering the picture in all your blundering innocence, may well be the catalyst for some long-awaited climax, or the last in a series of minor but incessantly accumulating, and finally back-breaking, straws. Especially if you have done something to engage the interest of that person. We are quick to incorporate other people into our dramas if they 'interest' us. It happens without thinking.

So that I now have to place that enhanced, glamorised version of myself not in some otherwise calm and neutral context, but in a context of already intense emotional upheaval. Just as the fiancé disappears (whether banished or withdrawing), leaving behind a lover-shaped void in Nasreen's psyche, so this semi-hallucinated image of myself re-emerges in her life, already cloaked in the authority of his prior role as her approving teacher and now, as he deigns to enter into correspondence with her on equal terms, unwittingly making himself a natural target for the projection of further imaginary garlands and embellishments.

Pure conjecture, of course, and it feels very strange to be talking about myself as this supernatural figure, but it does go some way to explaining the early, relatively harmless phase of her interest in me. The flirting, the nervous self-commentary, the strange outburst of jealousy concerning her former classmate, all make a bit more sense in the light of this boosted, exaggerated version of reality

And finally I must go back to that momentous yet oddly muted meeting of ours at the cafe – 'sNice – where Nasreen came to give me her manuscript. Her subdued manner (in sharp contrast to the exuberant emails she had been sending) seems, in the light of these suppositions, less that of an innate 'reticence' than of the tongue-tied devotee overwhelmed by the presence of the object of both her reverence and her desire. In which case, as I begin blathering on about my apartment and the problem of finding another subtenant to share it with, it becomes possible, just, to imagine her in a state of confusion in which the distorting forces of merciless self-doubt and groundless optimism (both of which, from my own experience, form part of the turbulent atmosphere of an infatuation) mingle in such a way as to make her believe I am hinting that I would like her to become my subtenant, my secret apartment-sharer, with all the erotic promise such a hint implies, and thereby confirming her strong wish, her determination one might almost say, that I should be as interested in her as she is in me.

Whether or not this in fact represents what she believed at the time, later emails indicate that she subsequently decided to interpret my words in this way. But I'm inclined to think it *was* what she believed at the time. A firm belief in the existence of a reciprocal erotic attraction between us would explain her curious insistence that I was in love with her and unhappily married, despite my very clear assurances to the contrary, and would further account for her jealousy of her classmate, not to mention her delirious reaction to my question about veils.

So much for Nasreen's possible versions of me and the role these might have played in preparing the events that followed. But what of the role played by my versions of *her*? Did I bring nothing to the encounter, no half-finished narratives of my own, into which I might have knowingly or unknowingly incorporated her? Was I an objective, impartial observer, a purely neutral participant in those early months of our exchange?

I was not. Nobody ever is.

I mentioned a cross-country train ride that I took in the summer of 2006. This too was an event I perhaps glossed over a little hastily, especially given Nasreen's suggestion that I smuggle her along for the ride in my 'roomette'. Not that anything very dramatic happened on the journey, but it occurs to me that it might lend itself to the difficult task I now face of providing some kind of self-portrait, or at least an account of the various strivings and vexations that comprised my sense of who and what I was during that first phase of my encounter with Nasreen, and of what I myself brought to the encounter.

The purpose of my trip was to get to LA, where I had a journalistic assignment. I could have flown, but I had some time on my hands and wanted to see some of the country. Originally I had planned to go by Greyhound bus, but then I found out about the much more comfortable-sounding Superliners and decided to go by train instead. I had also discovered that one of the routes I could choose from passed through Santa Fe, which would allow me to visit the Kiowa Ranch, where D. H. Lawrence lived on and off during the last years of his life and where his ashes were brought after he died. Lawrence's novella *St Mawr*, to which I had recently written an introduction, is partly set at the ranch, and I was curious to see the place.

The journey begins on 8 June, which happens to be my forty-eighth birthday. The first night is on a regular train from Albany to Chicago (the Superliners don't come east of Chicago). The train is full – reservations only and no double seats available. I find myself next to a man in a linen jacket, wearing strong cologne. For an hour or so I pore over the *New York Times* and the *London Review of Books*: an article about an ocean of sand spreading across western China; a profile of Abu al-Zarqawi, the leader of al-Qaeda in Iraq who was killed yesterday by American forces; a story about a British subject tortured by the CIA with the apparent consent of MI5 agents, who visited him in his cell but did nothing to help.

A cell phone starts flashing through the breast pocket of my neighbour's jacket. He pulls it out and answers it, speaking at high speed in a language I don't understand.

I wander up to the cafe car and eat dinner. Back in my seat I take out a notebook and start working on a poem. It's about my father; one of several I have been trying to write since his death a few years ago, most of them in one way or another airing both my grief and my sense of the paltriness of my accomplishments compared with his (at my age he was designing, among other things, Britain's National Theatre). In this one I am trying to do something with an image of the invasive red-berried vine called bitter-sweet that has come in under the fence of my vegetable garden. When I started pulling it out I saw that it had spread dense clusters of tiny red roots deep into the garden itself and was going to be extremely difficult to get rid of. The sight of these roots had made me think of the dark crimson capillaries in my father's high-coloured cheeks (he looked like a freshly shaved Father Christmas), which in turn made me think of his presence in my mind, as warmly vivid since his death as it was when he was alive, and in particular of the conviction he appears to have bequeathed me that the only thing worth doing in life is to create art: high, serious art, uncompromised by any conscious striving for worldly success (a conviction that would be a lot easier to live with if he had also passed on the genius necessary to put it into practice).

I write the following lines (and I permit myself the bad form of

quoting my own words because they too are in due course to become exhibits in my antagonist's indictment against me, her fugue
of hatred, though it may be puzzling, just now, for the reader to understand how they could ever lend themselves to such a use):

> In your book, success
> was a dirty word, wealth
> even dirtier, fame
> not to be uttered;
> the work was all that mattered.
> I took that to heart I guess,
> in my own monkish fashion:
> 'So much to say no to
> before you can start to say yes'
> having long been my motto.
> No, for instance,
> to the bittersweet
> I'm trying to extirpate
> from under the garden fence . . .

At which point, having been fairly pleased with my progress, I suc-
cumb to doubts. Why should anyone but me be interested in these
intimate, personal matters? Shouldn't I be addressing the kinds of
self-evidently important subjects I was reading about in the papers
earlier on?

It is a recurrent anxiety of mine, this fear of irrelevance, and I
have no argument against it other than the fact, hardly an argument, that sometimes the urge to write these very private things is
stronger than the doubts about whether they are worth writing. Right
now, the doubts have become stronger than the urge and I close my
notebook. Gazing out past my cologne-scented neighbour at twilit
pastures, I try to salvage the wasted time by cooking up a story in

my head that will involve terrorists, CIA torturers, MI5 observers, and a showdown in the sand-drowned landscapes of western China. It seems to me that if I was to make a concerted effort – read some books, maybe take a research trip – I could possibly come up with something. But for reasons I don't fully understand I have a strong private taboo against such exercises: stories that owe their existence to an act of will rather than an irresistible internal necessity. What I would like ideally (embarrassing as it is to admit to such yearnings) would be for precisely that force, that 'irresistible internal necessity', to compel me to write about those large subjects instead of the subjects it does compel me to write about, though for this to happen, an event from that larger world would have to impinge directly on my life, and for *that* to happen I must either venture out of my fortress in the hope of something befalling me, or else wait patiently for someone or something to burst in through my door. The latter seems to me the more honourable option, but it requires more faith than I possess (why should any large subject come to my door?), and so I go out from time to time, as I am now: reluctantly, and full of misgivings about the validity of even so passive an exercise in self-exposure.

My neighbour glances at me. Seeing that I am doing nothing, he strikes up conversation. He is travelling to Toledo, he tells me, where he owns a men's clothing store. His voice, now that he is speaking English, is deep and mellifluous. Memory wants to place a moustache on his lip, but I took notes about his appearance and there is no record of a moustache. He is square-shouldered with large, square-tipped, well-manicured hands and neatly brushed black hair. A faintly dissatisfied expression hovers over him as we talk, the ghost of a frown at his dark brow, as if he is contemplating some vague, constant grievance while simultaneously trying to dismiss it.

He was born in Egypt, he tells me, and lived for several years in Europe – Belgium, Germany, Romania – before moving to the States.

I remark that it must be hard, right now, being an Egyptian in America. He shrugs, not disagreeing but not, apparently, regarding the matter as of any great importance. But then he nods. Yes, it can be hard, sometimes, but it's still a better life here than anywhere else. In Europe, he says, people wouldn't speak to him. His phrase has a dignified pathos about it: 'They did not want to speak to me.'

Darkness has fallen and the passengers in the seats around us are preparing for sleep: spreading coats on their knees, turning off overhead lights. Suddenly a blue blaze flashes from my neighbour's chest: the phone in his breast pocket pulsating again, brighter now, in the dimming carriage – a strange sight, as if his heart were throbbing with light. He answers it, speaking again at high speed in that harsh tongue – Egyptian Arabic presumably – that sounds to me like some plectrumed instrument being played with sudden, savage virtuosity. Listening, noting my own reactions, I remember the words of Frantz Fanon, drilled into me by an idealistic schoolteacher: 'It is necessary at all times and in all places to make explicit, to demystify, and to harry the insult to mankind that exists in oneself.' Well, I have made explicit to the best of my ability, I have demystified and diligently harried, but there are still things that evade my precautions, and the sounds of certain languages appear to be among them. I don't think I am alone in this. My own language, the Queen's English, is well known to strike the ear of many people as intrinsically offensive; the aural essence of officiousness and pomposity. And it isn't that I find my neighbour's language offensive; as a matter of fact I find it enviably expressive, but try as I might I cannot dispel the impression it arouses in me of violent emotion, as if in switching to it the man has jumped from the bland, have-a-nice-day conventions of American social interaction into a world of operatic amazements and outrages, every word its own little melodrama. Or as if the language were a force in itself, expressing its character through the man, making him its instrument. And at a certain point my

73

mind, acting in that solicitously associative manner mimicked so cleverly by online shopping sites ('since you looked at this you may also be interested in this'), calls up for consideration the stories I was reading earlier, about Abu al-Zarqawi, killed yesterday with his wife and child, and before I can catch myself (the mind has a mind of its own) I am back in the nightmarish aura of this figure who kidnapped and cut off the head of the American businessman Nicholas Berg with a knife while he – al-Zarqawi – and his four cohorts in ski masks and shemaghs shouted *Allahu Akbar*, God is Great, after which they posted a video online of the butchering, complete with the victim's screams, bearing the title 'Abu Musa'b al-Zarqawi Slaughters an American'. It isn't difficult to understand how a person becomes a terrorist: how, under what conditions, one might contemplate killing the representatives, military or even civilian, of forces fundamentally opposed to one's own existence. But to fall on the neck of a captive human being and hack off his head with a knife while he screams; to make yourself into the throat-ripping fiend of primeval nightmare, the crouching, leaping enemy of man, and then blazon images of the deed across the Internet; that would seem to shift the terms of conflict altogether out of the plane of human meaning – politics or even war – into some non-human dimension, bestial but also demonological, something like that realm of frenzied encounter imagined by medieval painters in their depictions of hell, the sinners torn apart by devils, the devils no less tormented-looking than their victims.

The phone call ends. We resume our conversation for a while, and then he yawns and closes his eyes and falls asleep.

In the small hours of the night we are woken – he and I – by federal agents carrying long black flashlights. They want our IDs, just his and mine. We hand them our driver's licences. After inspecting them and asking some cursory questions about our respective journeys, they leave. It is no big deal and neither of us makes any comment. But someone in our compartment must have alerted the guard to the presence of suspicious Middle Easterners on the train, presumably after hearing the man talk on the phone. Whoever it was apparently considered me just as suspicious as him, and I am glad of this, but even so I feel implicated: embarrassed and a little ashamed of what was going on in my mind while he was talking, the feverish drift of my thoughts, and as he returns his driver's licence to his wallet and buttons up his linen jacket again, I find myself attributing that restless, faintly injured look of his to an intuition about the nature of those thoughts, the way I mingled his image with that of the terrorist al-Zarqawi. One has no control over the use other people make of one's image or the sound of one's voice or any other outward manifestation of oneself. It is purely a matter of trust, and I feel, vaguely, that I have betrayed that trust. And I find myself wondering about some of the attitudes that survive in my mind: ruins of ancient prejudices, inactive but disturbing to encounter, like the decommissioned artillery emplacements we came across the following year in France, steel and concrete structures left behind by Mussolini's army in the woods above the Roya Valley in Provence, ilex growing out of the gun embrasures, earth silting up the inner chambers.

At 5 a.m. we pass oil refineries glittering in the dawn light, their domed tanks and flaring towers filigreed over in silver pipes, and then cross the Maumee River into Toledo, where my neighbour gets off, frowning again as he nods goodbye.

A woman takes his place. Fifties, puffy-eyed, eager to talk. She's on her way to a blues festival in Grant Park, tremendously excited about it. She works in a Michelin factory, also a source of great excitement (she's a type I've encountered before in America: the exuberant self-spokesperson who addresses you as if from an inner press conference in which you are the horde of journalists besieging her with questions). 'I used to build tyres,' she informs me. 'Any more I mainly just balance 'em.' She has two years to retirement, after which she plans to move somewhere with a better climate, 'somewhere you don't can get sunburnt and frostbit on the same day'. Noting her way with words, and mindful of my professional obligation to be interested in such things, I try to keep up a conversation with her, but I am still drowsy and there is something encroaching on my thoughts, some presence drawing them towards it, and I begin to feel my attention drifting.

I close my eyes. The feeling of being able to go back to sleep in the morning, after you have woken up, is one I associate with being young, when it was followed by my most memorably pleasant dreams: dreams of flying and then, later, erotic dreams. Even now it is a time of unguarded semiconsciousness, and I am only half aware that the presence drawing me pleasantly towards itself is Nasreen's.

A sexual overture, however firmly resisted, is registered in a part of the psyche that has no interest at all in propriety or fidelity or any other such considerations. If the person making the overture is attractive and interesting, then that part of the psyche regards it as a matter of course that you will go ahead and sleep with them, and in fact regards it as a deeply unnatural act to choose not to. Monogamous relationships require such unnatural acts to be committed from time to time, and so this is nothing new to me. But they have their reverberations nevertheless, and as daybreak rouses me out of this half sleep, a thought I have been reluctant to acknowledge comes to me with sharp clarity, which is that if I had not been married, or if I had been less than happily immured in my own domestic existence, things might have developed in a very different way between me and Nasreen. It makes me wince a little to acknowledge this. But now, as I disentangle myself from her image, or the image I have created of her, I realise that the offer implicit in her suggestion that I bring her along for this journey, however jokey its intent, has had other effects besides making me feel that the time has come to be, as I had put it to myself, 'more explicitly discouraging'. It has made me susceptible to her as an object of fantasy.

I have three hours to kill in Chicago. I've never been here before, but I feel a connection to the place via my father's enthusiasm for it (the same kind of half-real, half-spurious connection I feel towards Persian culture). He came here on a honeymoon tour of America with my mother and was smitten by Louis Sullivan's skyscrapers, so much so that by the time I was born, the phrase 'Louis Sullivan's skyscrapers in Chicago' had become a permanent part of the verbal furniture of our household, and I grew up as familiar with it as I was with our sofas and chairs. At school or other places where I might want to impress people with my worldliness and culture I would casually utter it – *Louis Sullivan's skyscrapers in Chicago* – as if I had a natural right to speak of these buildings with my father's warmly proprietorial affection.

But in fact I have no idea which of these tall buildings surrounding me are Louis Sullivan's skyscrapers, and anyway the truth is I am not at ease thinking about architecture at all. Though he was the soul of tolerance in most respects, my father was something of a tyrant when it came to the visual arts, and I am still afraid of liking things he might turn out to despise (I was under a cloud for several years as a small boy for liking the garden gnomes outside a suburban house in Surrey), so I tend to wander around towns and cities in a state of paralysed judgement, aesthetically speaking, while other kinds of judgements and observations seethe inside me with a compensatory hyperactivity. To me, the half square mile of Chicago I explore feels much like other Midwestern cities I have visited – Minneapolis, Pittsburgh – the same gleaming blocks and towers with their chain restaurants and stores and cafes, all glazed in the peculiar high polish of the contemporary American mainstream that elides the buildings with the food, the commercial music, the movies, the magazines, in a single expression of the collective human will at its most dazzlingly efficient, which also, alas, by some odd quirk in the laws of existence, appears to be its most spirit-numbing, a reflection that surprises me as it breaks to the surface inside me, though before I can pursue it any distance I find myself brought up short by the familiar downward slippage in the tenor of my thoughts, and instead begin to question why so much of what I experience these days takes on this negated aspect; why, as I had put it in the poem I was trying to write (before it too became a victim of the very tendency it was trying to articulate), there seems to me to be 'so much to say no to / before you can start to say yes'. Or why, at least, this capacity for negation and rejection is not matched by an equal capacity for being gladdened and excited by things, as my father was, right to the end of his life. (The day he died, lying in hospital with pneumonia, he repeatedly asked his doctor if there was a chance, 'a sporting chance', that he might be able to take the trip he and my mother had arranged for the following week, to visit the castles of Oman.) I grew up expecting to be just like him, but I seem to be evolving in a different direction. In the past decade, especially, the spectrum of things capable of arousing a comparable enthusiasm in me seems to have narrowed steadily. Family, friends, a few books . . . not much else. And the things that do excite me tend to do so for reasons that seem vaguely pathological, morbid rather than uplifting; the interest itself more a state of passive enthralment than a matching, reciprocal energy. All decompositional forms and textures fascinate me – ruins, fall foliage, corrosion patterns, freaks and excesses of collapsing societies, stories of self-destruction through alcohol, drugs, sex – and I have come to think that I belong to the category of creatures that have an innate, organic affinity with the downward stroke of nature, the implosive cycle. The Zoroastrian religion of ancient Persia divided all phenomena into those that belonged to the creator, Ormuzd, and those that belonged to the destroyer, Ahriman. Bulls and fresh water belonged to Ormuzd; vultures, crocodiles and salt water to Ahriman. We grow up wanting to be creatures of Ormuzd, or I did: the writers I admired most at university, and still do – Tolstoy, D. H. Lawrence – were celebrators of life, growth, vitality, and my ambition was to be their heir. But what I look at so admiringly through their eyes has a way of turning to ashes when I look at it through my own. While I am reading, for instance, Lawrence's story 'Sun', in which a woman is liberated from the greyness of her domestic life in New York by a trip to Sicily, where she spends day after day lying naked in the sun, I am caught up unresistingly in the woman's ecstatic inner awakening. But after I have finished, a weariness comes over me and all I can think of is UV rays and ozone depletion and skin cancer. Even without such obvious grounds for scepticism, I find, when it comes to it, a layer of indifference between myself and the things I too would like to celebrate; a barrier that requires more and more effort to surmount. In this respect I tell myself I am, if nothing else, authentically of my time. Because if we are entering an age of losses, extinctions, elemental poisonings, gigantic simplifications and erasures – an entire age of Ahriman, in fact – then indifference would seem to be a necessary adaptive trait.

(I record these meanderings purely for the sake of the self-portrait that I am trying to paint here. They were the things that preoccupied me at that particular time.)

My Superliner, the Southwest Chief, is ready to board when I get back to the station. The chain of double-decker carriages lies along the platform like a glittering, recumbent blue-and-silver dragon, snoring in its berth. Childishly, I hope I am on the upper floor, and I am. My roomette is about seven feet long and three feet deep, with two seats facing each other beside a large window. The ends of the seats slide together to form a bed, and there is another bunk that folds down from the ceiling. It is functional but snug, something between a ship's cabin and a space capsule, with built-in drink holders and coat hangers and spotlights and a curtaining door that folds away into itself. I settle in with a feeling of pleasant loneliness and apprehension, as if I am embarking on something more unpredictable than a voyage along fixed steel rails.

We depart in the mid-afternoon, a slow grind through Chicago's suburbs and exurbs: Naperville, Mendota – places with names but no gaps between them, only denser entanglements of highways curling like gigantic spilt film reels. Miles and miles of new housing flow by in different stages of development: skeletons of golden lumber, entire half-finished towns wrapped in Tyvek, spanking new McMansions with their turrets and buttresses freshly painted mint and strawberry. These in particular, these kingly existences-in-waiting, acquire in recollection a look of melancholy eagerness as they stand in readiness to be owned and entered (melancholy because they may still be waiting: four years later, as I write, the economy is in ruins and everywhere you see unbought constructions from that time fading together in disappointed groups, dust in their virginal windows, the old meadows, of which they were, as the phrase goes, the 'last harvest', springing back up as crabgrass and goldenrod through cracks in their unused driveways).

It takes two hours before intervals of undeveloped land begin to appear, odd-looking at first, like oversights on the part of local planners, until, slowly, it's the factories and suburban houses that begin to look out of place, and then, as the evening comes in yellow and warm through the window, we curve out into the flat immensity of the prairie.

My phone rings: my son calling to say goodnight. Augustus (I'll call him that) is six. Our relationship is largely physical: mainly he likes to hurl himself at me with flailing fists and then be turned up-side down and swung around in circles. But he also likes to be read to, and for the past year I have been reading Tintin to him. I was a devoted reader of these books throughout my childhood and well into my adolescence, and even now my enjoyment of them is of a primary, rather than a nostalgic, nature. The line drawings seem richer every time I look at them, especially the night scenes with ocean liners or cars defined as solid blocks of black on midnight blue, backlit or shot through with yellow electric light, and the stories – comic, adventure-filled, but anchored in lovingly observed human behaviour – still move me.

But what has made the books so enduringly appealing to me is, I think, a purely accidental quality: the way their apparent Englishness is overlaid on an ineradicable foreignness. I had no idea the books were translations when I first started reading them, and by the time I discovered they were, it was too late for me to stop thinking of Tintin and his companions as English: English in a way that was at once deeply strange and soothingly familiar. They spoke English; their streets and signposts had English names; the countryside around Captain Haddock's home, Marlinspike Hall, looked just like the countryside around my parents' cottage in Sussex with its spin-neys and dovetailing fields. But of course they were all merely 'pass-ing' as English. Marlinspike Hall made a highly dubious English stately home, being, of course, a French chateau. The cars were on the wrong side of the road and as foreign-looking as the Citroën Safari my father drove through the lanes of Sussex, all curving proboscis. The policemen, when they arrived on the scene, wore odd, diminu-tive kepis on their heads instead of proper bobbies' helmets, and there were stripes down the sides of their trousers.

As the son of Jews who had joined the Church of England and then lapsed from that and now saw themselves as not quite English without being unimpeachably Jewish either, I was highly susceptible to these images of cheerfully imperfect assimilation. I felt at home in the not-quite-England they depicted, in a way that I never quite did in the real England, where, at the schools I attended, being of Jewish descent was more like a mild disability than something to be proud of or even indifferent towards.

None of which is of any consequence to Augustus, thank God, who likes the books for straightforward reasons, above all Captain Haddock's torrents of invective, which he reproduces faithfully at the top of his voice all day as he runs around the house: *Pockmark! Jellyfish! Bashi-bazouk!* (Now, older, he does the same, only with rap lyrics, inserting a silent beat for the 'fucker' part of 'motherfucker' if he thinks an adult may be listening, so that the songs sound like strange, hiccuping incantations to his mother.)

Since I can't read to him this evening, we talk about the books instead. I tell him I've just been in Chicago, the main setting for *Tintin in America*. It occurs to me that the developments I passed through earlier, with their look of having sprung up overnight, are just like the town Tintin passes through in that book, the one that springs up instantaneously around an oil prospector's freshly dis-covered gusher: banks and hotels fully built by noon, traffic lights, cops and zoning ordinances in place by mid-afternoon. But he is less interested in my analogy than I am and soon interrupts me, speaking in a Chinese accent, or at least his version of my version of a Chinese accent:

'I am going to cut off your head.'

The phrase startles me, though I recognise it at once. It comes from our favourite Tintin book, *The Blue Lotus*, or, as I have somehow permitted myself to call it, *The Brue Rotus*; regressing, in my son's company, to the soft racism that pervaded the world of my own child-hood, where nobody thought twice about mimicking foreign accents for a cheap laugh. The Tintin books, being all about encounters with foreigners, encourage this kind of low humour when it comes to reading them aloud. They contain a great deal of the comic racial stereotyping characteristic of their time. Being of my own time, I have felt obliged to talk about this with my son, explaining to him that the comedy is OK only because it is directed equally at all cultures, including Tintin's own, and because it is also largely without malice.

I eat a dinner of roast chicken and green beans, then sit for a while in the Observation Lounge, a glass-walled car with seats angled along the sides for optimal viewing.

We have entered a realm of white clapboard farmhouses, each grouped with its barn and silos in a palisade of shade trees, each surrounded by flat, immaculately tended fields of crops. The image repeats itself for mile after mile: farmstead and fields, farmstead and fields, the conformity of the pattern almost as impressive as its extent, as if some gigantic roll of wallpaper were unfurling at the same speed as our train, imposing its slightly surreal pastoral vision over the world with a gently irresistible power, like the power of sleep.

I am going to cut off your head . . .

My son's unabashed Oedipal exuberance comes back to me as I stare out. Something, some connected thought or memory, seems to be hovering behind the phrase, but I can't immediately grasp it.

I do remember that the words are spoken by a pleasant, educated young man, the son of Tintin's Chinese friend Mr Wang, who has been sent by his father to protect Tintin in Shanghai but has been poisoned with Rajaijah juice on his way.

Rajaijah juice is the poison of madness. It releases impulses of a violent but also childish nature (victims are as likely to spout nonsense or tweet like a bird as attempt to behead someone), and it is irreversible. I recall the picture of the sword-wielding young man in his tunic and skullcap, grinning cheerfully as he grabs Tintin by the shoulder and tells him: *I am going to cut off your head . . .*

The phrase revolves in my mind, trailing various associations. Abu al-Zarqawi, of course, and the many other educated young men you read about all the time now who have drunk the poison of madness and slipped back into the realm of boyhood fantasy, no longer inhibited from speaking its elemental language of explosion and decapitation. I think of the trance-like dance my son calls 'exploding', in which he hurls himself up and down on our bed or on the trampoline out in the yard for hours at a time, flinging his arms in the air and tossing his head back with a rapturous expression while making sounds of bomb blasts, rattling gunfire, swishing light sabres, lost in an imaginary world of blissful, unending combat. I think of Osama bin Laden's favourite saying from the Prophet (so I read somewhere): 'I wish I could raid and be slain, and then raid and be slain, and then raid and be slain'; its recognition of bodily ecstasy as the secret basis of terror, with even an infantile eroticism implicit in the lullaby rhythms (bin Laden could be the dead man in my fable, my underworld double, born the same year as me, father a builder of monuments, himself a dreamy, retiring type, living for a time in his agrarian idyll with vague pretensions to poetry until he found his true vocation). But none of this quite brings me in reach of whatever it was I had felt hovering in the aura of that phrase, and I get up, walking back to my roomette with the thwarted feeling that comes when you fail to find your way into some glimpsed area of thought that had seemed to promise a spell of pleasurable contemplation.

Now it is twilight and again the landscape has changed. Different shades of green tinge the grey shadows, and the country has a gentle roll in it, with woods and streams curving down into pockets of darkness. It reminds me of England: an improbably unspoiled England, with shire-sized vistas stretching away like old ink-tinted maps of English hunting country. Only the strange bluish greens and the tall pewter towers of the grain silos (fewer and farther between now) strike a foreign note, though the effect of them, like the kepis and peculiar cars in Tintin, isn't so much to cancel the impression of Englishness as to suggest an Englishness under some interestingly sinister enchantment.

There is a knock at my door: one of the train conductors, come to prepare my bed for the night. I stand to the side, watching her fold the seats together.

'What state are we in?' I ask.

She turns to face me, a pleasant-looking woman in her thirties, with a lock of gold hair curling from under her grey Amtrak visor.

'Missouri,' she says.

She gives me a smile, as if ready to talk more if I would like to. I *would* like to, but I am distracted by something and she leaves before I can speak.

And then, as she disappears down the corridor, I catch hold of what was eluding me before. It was possibly the knock at the door that reminded me, because that is how the adventure begins: a disturbance in the doorway on New Year's Eve as the stranger bursts into the castle, cantering into the banquet hall on a horse. In one hand he holds a branch of holly, in the other a massive axe. He himself is enormous, a giant of a man, and his beard is green.

It occurs to me as I write that even then, at this early, not yet hostile stage in Nasreen's campaign, I *was*, after all, aware that some large subject had arrived at my own fortress door, despite my scepticism about the likelihood of such a thing ever happening. It was just that the nature of the challenge she represented hadn't yet disclosed itself. The Green Knight's challenge is of course immediate and unambiguous: the most bizarre challenge in all of literature, and also, in its sheer brazen irrationality, a radical summation of all other challenges. I will stake everything and lose everything if you will stake everything and lose everything and then perhaps one or both of us may gain something neither had ever imagined even existed.

You cut my head off, he says to Sir Gawain, offering him the axe, and in a year and a day's time, seek me out and let me do the same to you.

I was thirteen, in my last year at boarding school, when I first read *Sir Gawain and the Green Knight*. It was given to our class by our English and music teacher, an enthusiast for all things medieval. The school itself, a Gothic pile rising from the greensward of its golf course and games fields, had something medieval about it. All boys, its atmosphere was part monastery, part military outpost. Before meals we lined up in divisions for inspection, and then marched in formation into a dining hall frescoed from top to bottom in scenes from Arthurian legend, with castles, forests, jousting knights and a gold-hilted sword in a stone.

Free time was devoted largely to warfare. In the woods beyond the games fields we built fortified encampments over the craters left by fallen trees, digging trenches and tunnels between them to create ever-larger compounds, and charging out to attack other boys' encampments (to raid and be slain, and then raid and be slain) with pine-cone hand grenades and, when we could smuggle them past the matrons who checked our baggage on arrival every term, pea-shooting Sekiden guns.

There was the physical joy of fighting, but more intense and long-lasting was the glory that burned inside you when you had distinguished yourself by some bold act and been recognised for it. In the austere regime we lived under, with few possessions and no personal power, glory was what made us rich, and we attended to the correct remembrance of our own and one another's deeds with the heraldic zeal of Arthur and his knights.

There was a chapel too, a small stone and stained-glass building, which you entered through a door in the gym, exchanging the thick sock-stink for the scent of candle wax. A portrait of Edmund the Martyr, for whom the school was named, was painted over the nave. The school motto – *Per Manendo Vincimus*, 'Through perseverance we conquer' – was inscribed above the altar on a pennant with a stylised flutter in it rather like the one adopted after 9/11 for depictions of the American flag; that stirring, menacing, triple ripple suggestive of some violent agitation being stoutly withstood by its fabric. Every weekday morning we filed in for prayers, Christians and heathens alike (the King of Jordan's son, Prince Abdullah, now king himself, sat in the pew behind me with his bodyguards), and on Sundays there was a full-length Communion service, also obligatory.

I didn't mind this; in fact I liked it. I joined the choir and wore my white surplice with modest pride. I liked being part of the mood of gentle pathos created by the anthems we sang: 'Ave Verum', 'O for the Wings of a Dove', and I liked the religion too, or thought I did. When the chaplain commended us to the Peace of God which passeth all understanding I felt a soothing calm settle over me. If I was unhappy I said the Lord's Prayer and felt happier. It seemed to me a natural progression from this to partaking in the Communion itself, and I signed up for confirmation classes so that I could join the other initiates at the altar, consuming the wafers and wine.

And yet almost from the beginning of these classes, a feeling of unease began mounting inside me. I tried to ignore it, but a few weeks before the Bishop of Chichester was due to arrive and perform the ceremony, it rose to a pitch of intense, if obscure, dread. Bracing myself for an unpleasant encounter, I told the chaplain I was having doubts, and after a surprisingly short conversation (he didn't seem nearly as concerned or upset as I felt he should have been, or as I was myself), I pulled out. Sometimes, looking back, I have been tempted to see this episode as the sign of some authentic core of Jewishness in my soul, recoiling from the act of apostasy. But aside from the fact that none of those things mean very much to me any more – souls, apostasy, authentic cores – the truth was that I experienced it as something purely negative; merely a kind of surging veto, unaccompanied by any more positive sense of who or what I might be if I was not this.

All of which – the medieval atmosphere, the strong group identity and my dawning sense of estrangement from it, also the near total absence of women (and its effect of investing the female sex with powers verging on the occult) – made me naturally inclined to be interested in a text like *Sir Gawain and the Green Knight*. Even so, I was unprepared for the force of its impact on me. Aside from anything else, it was the first piece of literature that made me want to write something myself. The speed and boldness of its opening moves excited me like nothing I had read before. There was something almost physically violent in the way the story accelerated into high gear through those first outrageous images – the green-bearded knight on his green horse, the beheading, the monstrous body seizing its own head and riding off – the alliterative lines slashing their way forward as if the act of creation were occurring over a simultaneous hidden act of destruction. I had noticed that when my father was pleased about the way his work was going, a look of savage glee (I think of it as his 'Tartar' expression – his ancestors were Russian) would light up his face, and I connected that expression with this opening, each seeming to reveal something pleasurably violent at the core of the creative act: a sensation I was extremely interested in experiencing myself.

But even more stirring than this literary pleasure was my feeling of affinity with the figure of Gawain himself.

From his first moment of modest self-assertion as he asks King Arthur's permission to accept the Green Knight's challenge, I identified with him in a peculiarly intimate way. Even now, at different moments of my life, different junctures of the strange quest that follows (strange because it is the story of a man seeking his own destruction) seem to throw an uncanny light on my own existence.

Permission granted, he takes the axe and prepares to deal the blow. The knight bares his neck and Gawain strikes, cutting the great head clean from the massive shoulders.

Does he believe the affair is now over, that the decapitated knight, having made his foolish provocation and got what he asked for, is going to remain obligingly dead? If so, he is seriously mistaken. Blood spurting from the wound, the Green Knight picks up his rolling head by the hair and remounts his horse. 'Find me at the Green Chapel,' he says, angling his disembodied face at Gawain. He gives no clue as to where, in all of England, this chapel might be, but warns Gawain that if he fails to come, he will be called a coward. (I want to write that as 'a fucking faggot coward' but the text won't quite bear me out.)

Life, death, honour, reputation. Such, at this point, are the terms and stakes of the challenge.

The story has been light-hearted up until now. Christmas festivities are in full swing and laughter pervades the court. But as the year passes and the time approaches for Gawain to set off on his mission, anxiety descends. For Gawain's sake his comrades keep up the pretence that this is all a jolly adventure, but under their jokes they are already grieving for a doomed man.

There is an icily ironic scene of him putting on his sumptuous armour, the last word in sabots and greaves, all lavishly embossed and embroidered, with the pentangle, symbol of virtue and purity, painted in gold on the shield. The irony being that his mission is to receive a blow, not to ward one off, so that all of this extravagant protection is entirely pointless. This is a suicide mission,

Off he rides then, setting out into the wide reaches of prehistoric Britain. Loneliness assails him. Hunger sets in. Cold pierces through his armour, and as the appointed day approaches with him still having no clue as to the chapel's whereabouts, he begins to reckon with the gravity of his situation. The isolation of the hero has begun. As he sleeps in his armour, near slain with sleet, night after night in the naked rocks with the cold creeks clattering around him, his severance from the easy, cosy, determinedly upbeat collective consciousness of the court is complete, and he begins to emerge as an individual human being, 'a man all alone': vulnerable, doubting, with failure and dishonour looming, and annihilation suddenly an encroaching reality.

In this condition, lost in a deep wood, he reverts, as people do, to the self-soothing formulas of religion. He says his Lord's Prayer and his Ave Maria, then begins making the sign of the cross over himself, once, twice, three times . . .

A castle appears, shimmering through the oaks. I remember it as I remember the town that springs up instantaneously in Tintin, or the McMansion developments outside Chicago, with their look of improbable newness. To Gawain it resembles a paper ornament, with its shining white towers.

At the entrance he calls out and a porter comes, welcoming him as if he is expected. The lord of the castle, Sir Bertilak, another gigantic man, though with a red beard rather than a green one, greets him warmly and has his servants show him to a luxurious bedroom with all the latest conveniences, including a curtained four-poster bed. After he has washed and changed he is brought to a feast in a hall with a roaring fire. On learning his name, the assembled guests go into little ecstasies of flattery. He has a reputation, he discovers, for fine speech, and the guests declare themselves thrilled at the prospect of such a paragon joining them for their Christmas revels. He will tutor them, they chorus obsequiously, in the correct use of words, and by his example he will teach them love-talking, 'luf-talkyng': the language of flirtation and Courtly Love, in which he is also, so he learns to his surprise, a renowned expert. (I remember an early email from Nasreen in which she mentions she has heard I have a reputation as a ladies' man, with lots of 'wild girls' in my past. Since she knew nobody from my past, I understood this to be pure invention, part of her campaign of flirtatious ego massage. It didn't occur to me to wonder whether her cavalier way with the concept of 'reputation' might turn out to have a less benign side.)

No sooner is the theme of 'luf' announced than Gawain glimpses an attractive young woman: his host's wife, as it happens, on her way into midnight mass. He follows after her into the castle chapel. During the service she turns from her private pew to glance at him, and you can feel the electric jolt pass between them as she lets him gaze a moment on her delicate beauty.

The next day is Christmas, and he sits beside the young woman at the banquet. The two take a keen pleasure in each other's company, talking quietly together in a private exchange that the author describes as a sweet dalliance, a 'dere dalyaunce', though he also assures us, with only the lightest touch of irony, that it is irreproach-able: 'closed fro fylthe'; a minor paradox that captures perfectly the ambiguous nature of any flirtation in its early stages, where nothing unequivocal has yet been said.

Courtly Love, that elaborate medieval attempt to reconcile raw desire with the smooth running of the social machine, is in fact a deliberate exercise in such ambiguities. Under its rules a young knight may fall in love with a married woman and enter into the steamiest of flirtations with her, in which everything is permitted except for the ultimate consummation. The beauty of the formula is that it appears to acknowledge both the force of lust and the virtue of fidelity. Like all codes of sexual conduct, it is fatally flawed, the state of deferred gratification being naturally unstable, and therefore highly likely to culminate in tragedy or farce. But it has an appealing realism about it, and at least tries to recognise the human psyche in all its contradictory totality.

The Green Chapel turns out to be just two miles from this castle, which means Gawain can stay on in comfort until New Year's Day. To pass the time till then, Sir Bertilak suggests a game: he will go out hunting with his men every day while Gawain stays behind, relaxing at the castle, and every evening they will exchange whatever each has gained during the day.

And so now the story begins to close in on its true quarry, shifting its hero away from the familiar clarities of valour and physical action into the more treacherous realm of psychological and moral combat.

The first morning, while Sir Bertilak hunts deer, Gawain is woken by the sound of his bedroom door being quietly opened. Glancing through the curtains of his four-poster, he sees his host's wife, lovely as ever, coming into the room. Locking the door behind her, she lifts the curtain of his bed and, to his great embarrassment, sits down beside him. A long, comically erotic scene of attempted seduction follows, in which the lady, full of jokes and teasing flattery (*eshveh, kereshmeh, naz*), tries to persuade Gawain to overcome his scruples and take advantage of her husband's absence. In very candid language she offers him her body to 'take his pleasure with' on the silk sheets of his bed. For all the light-heartedness, the stakes of the situation are high: declining a sexual advance requires great tact if you want to avoid giving mortal offence, while to accept it, however strong the temptation (and we can assume it is intense), would, in this instance, irreparably violate Gawain's sense of himself as an honourable human being. He acquits himself well, maintaining impeccable charm while getting the lady out of his chamber without yielding anything more serious than a single, chaste kiss.

This, as the game requires, he passes on to Sir Bertilak, in exchange for the venison his host has butchered that day.

But when an attractive person makes you an offer like this, she or he establishes a powerful link with your own psyche, and whether or not you are interested in pursuing it, a whole new world of erotic possibility has become, as I realised that morning, latently present in your imagination. Out of this virtual world arise the sweetest of dreams but also the succubi and demon-lovers of folklore and literature: Lilith and Lamia, Heathcliff and Peter Quint, all the phantasmal femmes fatales of Keats and Coleridge and the Pre-Raphaelites, and these visitants can be much harder to keep at bay than flesh-and-blood human beings, no doubt because their substance, such as it is, originates at least partly in oneself.

On the second day she comes again to his room, his roomette, her presence seeping in like a scent, only this time what is at stake is not just his self-regard, his image of himself as a Man of Honour, but something more like his soul; the author carefully recalibrating his description of the lady's softly insistent verbal blandishments to usher in the suggestion of a motive beyond love or even lust, namely the graver mission of 'winning him to wrong'.

And this time she seems stronger than before; bolder, more laughingly insistent, the labyrinths of her conversation as she begs him to take her on as his private student ('teach me', she says, 'while my husband is away') more elaborately carnal, as if that single kiss the morning before, chaste as he had believed it to be, had provided her with some vital nourishment. Again he resists her, but you can feel his pleasure in her nearness working on him, filling him with a dangerous confidence in his ability to have it both ways: enjoy the situation (he is much more wittily poised in his repartee this time) while keeping it under control, which he does, though this time he rationalises the yielding of not one but two kisses before the session comes to an end, and one knows, by the logic of trifold escalation common to all such stories, that something fateful is going to happen next time she comes to visit.

It is night-time now, and we have just crossed the Kansas River. In Kansas I fall into a deep sleep, rocked by the rhythms of the train, and in the morning we are still (such is the scale of things here) in Kansas.

But the green has gone from the country and the plain looks seared brown. For a long time it is flat and absolutely featureless. I eat breakfast and wander on down to the Observation Lounge. It is crowded despite the early hour: people staring out of the windows, others hunched over electronic devices, the machines tweezling and winking alertly, the humans bleary and rumpled.

An industrial dairy operation goes by with thousands of Holstein cows penned into brown dirt feedlots. Some of the lots have artificial mounds in them, on which the cows lie curled up asleep like ungainly black-and-white cats. Soon after that we come to Dodge City, where a group of scouts boards the train. One of them sits next to me, a boy of sixteen or so, grey-eyed, round-faced, lividly acned. With a congeniality that seems precocious even in this land of easy openness, and downright defiant in one so incandescently spotty, he immediately strikes up conversation. He and his troop are on their way to New Mexico for a camping trip in the mountains. He himself has never left Kansas before and never seen a mountain. He speaks with a long-ago twang like a farm boy in an old movie:

'Ain't never seen a mountain before . . .'

He's adopted, grew up with his cousins, a family of nine kids.

'There's a lot of us so we don't have much money,' he informs me, another of these diligent self-spokespersons, strongly conscious of his place in the American epic. The family used to have a big farm where he would ride around all day on horseback. Now they have just fifteen acres and some livestock. He breaks the horses, a dangerous business.

'I lost count how many bones I've broke.'

Every time he finishes talking he purses his lips as though literally, thriftily, closing up some coin-filled purse.

A small rise appears in the distance. He turns to me.

'Would that be considered a mountain?'

'No.'

Farms glide by, with pale green irrigation circles on the brown dirt and trailers for the workers. We follow a creek, its banks lined with what I am guessing from the hair-like stuff in their branches must be cottonwoods. A wrecked barn stands alone, broken beams angling frenziedly skyward.

'Tornado done that,' the boy says, pursing his lips.

Long miles of empty sagebrush pass, then a squat, windowless building, surrounded by razor-wire fencing. The boy grins:

'Prison.'

One of his brothers is a prison guard. Not in this particular prison, but it would seem all prisons are looked on fondly as a result of the connection. The family likes to amuse itself by asking this brother what he is going to do when he has to lock up a relative.

'He says he'll just slam the door on 'em a little harder than he usually does. Couple of our cousins might be landing there pretty soon I reckon.'

Another bump appears on the flat plain.

'Would *that* be considered a mountain?'

'Not really.'

'Highest thing I ever seen.'

I look at him, wondering if he's putting me on, but he seems sincere.

Later in the day mountains do finally become visible in the

distance, but by then he has gone off somewhere, so I miss his reaction. A person crosses your path; briefly their story intersects with yours and then diverges again, leaving something of itself with you and maybe taking something of yours in return, and they're gone. These days I have to remind myself that encounters with other people can be both interesting and inconsequential.

Adobe churches and farm buildings appear. The train groans uphill to the Raton Pass, highest point of the trip. Soon after this we come to Lamy, the Santa Fe station, where I get off for my detour to D. H. Lawrence's ranch.

In the old East Germany a person who helped others escape over the Wall was called a *Fluchthelfer* – 'flight-helper'. If you read naively, as I mostly do, to make sense of your life, rather than for more sophisticated aesthetic or scholarly reasons, then certain writers inevitably become your own *Fluchthelfer*, helping you over your own walls, whether to escape reality or, as I prefer to see it, to find your way into it. For me D. H. Lawrence has always been such a writer. His best works, mainly the novellas and short stories, have the same imaginative audacity about them as *Gawain*, and give out the same exhilarating sense of old things – stale sentiments, defunct notions – being slashed and smashed as quickly as new things are being created. His statements about life and death, good and evil, men and women, all tossed out with a casually apocalyptic grandiosity, still stir me long after I have stopped 'agreeing' with most of them. 'Man must find a new expression, give a new value to life, or his women will reject him, and he must die.' 'Man, as yet, is less than half grown.' Man this, man that . . . not the kind of language we appreciate any more, and his reputation has accordingly suffered badly during the past decades. With my own recent interest in the processes by which reputations become tarnished (another of Nasreen's many legacies), I

96

have begun to find this aspect of Lawrence almost as fascinating as the writing itself, but back then, as I stepped out of the air-conditioned train into the furnace heat of the New Mexico June, it was simply as an admirer of his work.

I pick up a rental car in Santa Fe, and drive into the mountains towards Taos. It's too late to get to the ranch today and I spend the night in Taos itself, at an inn that was once the home of Mabel Dodge Luhan.

It was Mabel Dodge Luhan who brought Lawrence to New Mexico in the first place. There are books about both of them on a shelf in the lobby. After dinner I look through them, and before I know it I seem to be seeing yet another version of my own circumstances unfolding before me, projected through their intertwining lives.

She was in her early forties then, a wealthy heiress and patron of Native American art, with a colourful past that included several husbands and an attempt to commit suicide by eating figs mingled with broken glass. Having read a few of Lawrence's books, she had decided she needed him in her life – 'I wanted Lawrence to understand things for me' – and she set about enticing him to Taos. The year-long campaign featured letters filled with native American herbs, the gift of a supposedly enchanted necklace to Lawrence's wife, Frieda, and a determined effort of telepathic attraction: 'I'd sit there and draw him until he came' was how she remembered it. He resisted at first, travelling instead to Ceylon and Australia, but eventually the effort paid off, and he and Frieda arrived at Lamy station in September 1922.

Mabel, who had a husband of her own on the premises, immediately set about attempting to seduce her long-awaited visitor. She tried to convince him that his marriage had gone stale – 'You need something new and different . . .' – and after a while she persuaded him to work with her on, yes, a novel that she was trying to write

Was he attracted to her? The books don't say, but by the time of this proposed collaboration he had committed the indiscretion of criticising his wife to her, complaining about Frieda's 'heavy German hand', and this sounds to me like a man declaring himself available, at least theoretically, for a lighter, non-Germanic touch. Add to this the aura of scandal surrounding his name ever since his elopement with Frieda, a married mother of three, not to mention the contents of the books themselves with their celebration of the senses and emphasis on spontaneity in human relations, and you can easily imagine how Mabel might have thought an affair was a possibility.

She arranged a meeting to discuss her novel. For the venue, she selected the sun roof outside her bedroom. On the appointed day she led him upstairs, naked under her soft white cashmere wrap. As they passed through the bedroom itself, the sight of the unmade bed seems to have stirred an awareness in Lawrence of the possible seriousness of the situation he was getting himself into. He hesitates, embarrassed, evidently realising the moment has come to clarify his intentions – possibly as much to himself as to her. So once again we have the comical figure of the man in the bedroom, the boudoir, the roomette, being impinged on by the desires of a woman he is at least passingly attracted to, and making up his mind (perhaps a little culpably late in the proceedings) to keep her at arm's length. Comical because, although we may commend him for being a good husband and model citizen, we find him a bit ridiculous as a man, because what kind of man other than a priest or a jihadi really cares, on his *own* account, about protecting his chastity?

Not being a fictional character, he doesn't handle himself with quite the suaveness of Sir Gawain, but in his own way he seems, after all, to observe the same code of conduct as the virtuous knight:

'I don't know how Frieda's going to feel about this,' he mutters nervously.

98

Not exactly what you'd expect from the author of *Lady Chatter-ley's Lover* or the excoriator of Christianity who blamed Jesus for the calamitous ascendancy of the mind over the senses. *I don't know how Frieda's going to feel about this . . .* And yet one warms to him for it, or I do: a confused and conflicted human being like the rest of us. Future meetings are scheduled in his own quarters, with Frieda clumping noisily around close by, and the collaboration soon fizzles out.

In the morning I head up into the San Cristobal mountains to the Kiowa Ranch. Mabel, evidently generous as well as a good sport, deeded this property to the Lawrences after she realised she wasn't going to dislodge Frieda. The place, miles along a twisting red dirt road, is a jumble of modest wooden buildings with a disused corral below and Lawrence's memorial chapel on a hill above. Two sparrows are building a nest in an elk skull nailed to the fence of an overgrown garden; otherwise there are no signs of life. Near the main house is an enormous pine, leaning towards the rickety porch in the strong, steady wind. A sign warns you not to steal any of the pine cones strewn on the ground below it, and I realise this must be the great Ponderosa pine Lawrence describes in the finale of *St Mawr*, where the transfiguring description (his speciality was to describe something with vivid realism while at the same time trans-forming it into something else, basically whatever his argument at a given moment required it to be) turns the tree into an image of icy, swampy, pre-animal consciousness. I know the passage well: the tree standing like a demonish guardian, its pillar of flaky-ribbed copper rising in the shadows of the pre-sexual world, wind hissing in the needles, its cold sap surging and oozing gum, and the pine cones lying all over the yard, open in the sun like wooden roses.

There are hundreds of these 'wooden roses' lying all over the grass now, golden and enormous, ten times the size of any pine cone I have ever seen. I'm not, by nature, a souvenir hunter or collector of relics, and probably if there weren't the notice forbidding it, it wouldn't cross my mind to take one. But under the circumstances it is irresistible, and I place one furtively in my canvas shoulder bag.

A woman appears, grey-haired and sunburned. She must have come out of one of the other buildings. In her hand is a raspberry-red ice cream. I nod at her and she nods back. I'm not sure if she saw me stealing the pine cone.

'Nice day,' I say, feeling awkward.

'Yep.'

'Are you the caretaker?'

'Yep.'

'Can I . . . go inside the house?'

'Nope.'

'Oh. I guess I'll go see the chapel then.'

She says nothing. I walk up towards the chapel, feeling her eyes on me as I climb the zigzagging path up the hill.

The building is small and unpretentious, with a hand-hewn look that Lawrence would probably have approved of, the little rose window above the door just a truck wheel cemented into the white-washed wall. A clunkily sculpted phoenix squats on the roof. Inside, on the grey-tiled floor, is an altar with Lawrence's ashes mixed in the cement, also topped by a phoenix. The phoenix was Lawrence's personal heraldic emblem, his equivalent of Gawain's pentangle; fiery vitality being the principle he wished to live by, rather than Gawain's Christian morality (though he seems to have been wearing a pentangle in Mabel's bedroom). People have left small offerings on the altar – feathers, juniper berries, oak sprigs – which surprises me, imagining, as I somehow do, that I am the last living acolyte. I think of leaving the pine cone but find that I have already become too attached to the prospect of having it on my desk at home to contemplate sacrificing it.

On the wall is a framed official document from the US Consulate in Marseilles certifying that the ashes are those of David Herbert Lawrence, shipped to America aboard the SS *Conte di Savoia* along with the death certificate and cremation paperwork from the mayor's office in Vence, where Lawrence died of TB. Something about the display of this document, right here in the chapel, strikes me as overemphatic. The effect is to raise doubts where none might have existed otherwise. And as I read it I remember a story I had forgotten, which is that these are possibly not Lawrence's ashes in the altar here at all.

Frieda had a lover, an Italian infantry officer, Captain Ravagli, whom she married soon after Lawrence's death and sent to Europe to bring back the remains. But Ravagli, so the story goes, managed to leave the urn behind on a station platform, and brought home a substitute, filled with God knows what rubbish.

I am trying to enter into a properly receptive state of mind as I stand here in the chapel, but it is hard with the cruel comedy of this little fiasco echoing in the background of my thoughts. There is an amazing photograph of Frieda later on in her widowhood, ample and grey, with a cigarette dangling from the corner of her mouth, flanked by Mabel Dodge Luhan and Dorothy Brett, all three of them laughing. Brett was an English artist who lived here at the ranch with the Lawrences. It wasn't a *ménage à trois*, but she revered him and once, elsewhere, he did consent to go to bed with her, but couldn't get an erection (Brett remembers him shouting childishly, 'Your pubes are all wrong'), and I find myself thinking of that too, the photograph of the women who outlived their idol, joyous cackling survivor-laughs on their wrinkled faces, all of them no doubt glad, at some level, to be rid of this consumptive prophet with his spit and sputum and his everlasting exhortations and injunctions. Captain Ravagli probably would have suited them all much better: a robust, extrovert type, like the panther who takes the place of the tormented man starving himself to death in Kafka's 'A Hunger Artist'. Ravagli tried to read *Sons and Lovers* once, but didn't care for it: 'We don't need literature to know what to do' was his comment.

All of which, jostling in my head, is proving a considerable distraction. Here I am in the chapel, the holy of holies, braced for some kind of momentous reckoning with the great man, my own bearded giant (though he was physically small and went by Bert rather than Bertilak), but allowing myself to be sidetracked by these demeaning, unsubstantiated stories. I am singularly failing to rise to the occasion. Not only that, but in entertaining these slurs I have become complicit, it seems to me, in the general mockery that these days habitually greets Lawrence's name, even when there is a grudging acknowledgement of the acid brilliance of his prose. I, of all people, who unfailingly answer *St Mawr* when asked my favourite novel, and even once taught a class on it, proposing it as the only book ever written that convincingly imagines a state of happiness based on the real conditions of life, in all its destructiveness as well as its wild energy (the class wasn't a great success). And it hasn't escaped me either that these gossipy stories have in common the theme of emasculation, or, shall we say, betailing, as if there is something about the very presumption of a man trying to imagine, without irony, the condition of total fulfilment, emotional as well as sexual, that incites a jeering desire to see him impotent, cuckolded, cheated even of his own ashes. And here I am, his last disciple, with my own hand, as it were, on the gelding knife! I leave the chapel, dissatisfied with myself. As the line goes in the poem where Lawrence berates himself for throwing a log at a snake instead of seizing a rare opportunity to watch such a creature close up: 'I missed my chance with one of the lords of life.'

The caretaker is nowhere in sight as I drive off, and I take consolation in the thought that at least I have my wooden rose, my pine cone. Back on the train – a different train with different passengers but an identical roomette – I open my bag to gloat on it, thinking perhaps its talismanic powers will succeed where the chapel failed. Quite what form 'success' might take, I am not sure. A surge of creativity perhaps; inspiration for a poem or story, or just some phoenix magic to burn off the heavy vapours of Ahriman from my shoulders. Perhaps also I am half remembering the little pine cone hand grenades we used to hurl into one another's encampments at school, in which case there is possibly some idea of superior explosiveness attached to the object, of having got my hands on something incendiary enough to satisfy, once and for all, my desire to experience the pleasurable violence I have always felt to be present in the true creative act.

But whatever it may be I am not destined to find out. The pine cone isn't there. It appears to have fallen out of my bag somewhere en route.

Not a serious loss, I tell myself; not like losing a phone or a wallet. But I feel upset, even a bit crushed, as if I have been judged – or rather have somehow judged myself – unworthy of having it in my possession.

Somewhere after Albuquerque I go into the Observation Lounge. There aren't many free seats and without thinking I squeeze in next to a youngish guy, white, but dressed gangsta style in a filmy black do-rag, with a thin stirrup of beard around his jaw and chin. He mutters unpleasantly as I sit down, pointedly not moving his sprawled knee out of the space belonging to my seat. I try to ignore him but it is hard to concentrate on anything else in the presence of such open hostility. After a while he takes out a cell phone. I listen in while he arranges for a friend to wire him forty bucks to a Western Union in Los Angeles. In a quieter voice he jokes about having just got money out of a chick on the train who was hanging with him earlier.

He moves off after this but I see him again a few hours later at the bar, during a long wait at a station. He is talking with a girl who

I noticed boarding the train just a few minutes ago. She looks about eighteen: denim forage cap on her dyed black hair, heavily mascaraed blue eyes, close-fitting belly shirt. They appear to be flirting and I can't help feeling stunned at the speed with which he has moved in on her. While I watch them a voice comes over the PA: Would Michelle somebody or other please come down to the platform, where her dad would like to say goodbye to her? The girl gives a sour grin: 'Shit.' 'That you?' the guy asks her. 'Yeah.' 'You gonna go say goodbye?' 'No fuckin' way.' They laugh and go back to what they were talking about. After a couple more minutes the voice comes again: Would Michelle so-and-so please come down to the platform right away; her dad would really, really like to say goodbye to her. The girl rolls her eyes but again stands her ground, while the guy chuckles. I look at her, wanting to say something. She catches my eye. The guy turns, recognising me. He juts his chin as if to ask what the fuck am I looking at. I give a silent snort to show that I am not intimidated, but he has already turned back to the girl.

As I go back to my roomette the train pulls out and I wonder which of the three or four solitary men standing on the platform is the girl's father and what he could have done to deserve his daughter's treatment. My own daughter is ten, still entirely sweet-natured, and I dread even the most amicable distance opening between us, so I was feeling an instinctive solidarity with the girl's father and was wanting to urge her to say goodbye to him. Also as a father, I was feeling protective towards her, thinking I should warn her off this character who is apparently in the habit of fleecing unsuspecting girls on trains. But I was also – such is the riven nature of the psyche, or the male psyche, or anyway mine – looking at her with desires of my own, the soft clashing effect of nubile breasts aloft above a skeletal ribcage sharply alluring, and now, as I sit here back in my roomette, the awareness of this, mingling with the adrenalin still coursing through me from the man's aggression, and the attendant contradictory feelings of relief at having evaded violence and frustration at having been too well behaved or cowardly to inflict it, together have brought me into a place of familiar jangling confusion.

We are in the desert now. Vast pink-and-white-striped rock formations rise out of the cactus scrub like nature's own McMansions. I eat a solitary dinner, then turn in for the night. It takes me some time to fall asleep, and I sleep badly when I do.

On the third morning the mood shifts, ripening and sweetening, with a faint, premonitory sickliness about it: sin coming to fruition. She enters at dawn, naked under a fur robe, gems braided into her hair. Lying beside him in the curtained chamber, 'hir brest bare', she kisses him twice, bringing him into that state of arousal in which reason organises itself on a new basis and the arguments against consummation become harder and harder to remember. Here is a beautiful woman who wants you to make love to her. To refuse, to offend her as well as deny yourself the pleasure, strikes you as perverse, doltish, 'crathayn'. The ethical basis, the biblical idea of sin, asserts itself weakly in his mind, like the memory of a memory. She presses her advantage, gently twisting the moralistic language of his thoughts to promote her own gospel of love: 'Blame ye disserve, yif ye luf not that lyf that ye lye nexte.' Shame on you if you love not the living body by your side. He is perilously close to capitulation. And yet, contrary to expectation, he holds out once again. And this time the lady, planting a final kiss on his lips, ruefully concedes defeat.

But of course that isn't the end of the matter. Before she leaves, she unfastens her girdle, a cincture of green silk, and very touchingly asks her unyielding knight to accept it as a keepsake, a souvenir of their sweetly charged exchanges. Even this he attempts to refuse, but as he does so she plays her trump card, parrying him with the unexpected and, under the circumstances, extremely interesting information that this ghostly green shimmer, this near-virtual token of herself, happens to be endowed with magical properties, whereby no man who wears it may be cut down or killed. On learning this, our hero, who has spent a restless night dreaming of his imminent beheading, reveals at last a mortal flaw in his character: a willingness to cheat death. Sexual attraction alone may not have been powerful enough to win him to wrong, but that narrow form of desire is after all only a special instance of the desire for life itself (so the episode seems to be telling us), and this – the hope of warding off death, of arming himself with a talisman powerful enough to lift tomorrow's heavy sentence from his shoulders – is irresistible. He accepts the gift – how could he not? – without further argument. As the lady presses it into his hand, she begs him not to mention it to her husband, and he agrees, enmeshed already in the swiftly escalating logic of deceit.

So resilient, however, is his image of himself as a paragon of virtue and honour that for a time he succeeds in inducing a state of complete denial concerning his own deed. Hiding the girdle in his room, he goes to the castle chapel to make confession in preparation for the next day's ordeal, emerging as 'clene' – so the glintingly deadpan narrator assures us – as a shriven soul on judgment day, even though he hasn't said a word about his illicit possession of sorcerous materials or his intent to renege on the spirit, if not the letter, of his solemn covenant. And that evening, when he meets Sir Bertilak for the third exchange of spoils, he steps cheerfully forward to pass on his morning's harvest of kisses (Judas kisses, they inevitably seem at this point) without a word, or even a thought, about the densely potent garment secreted in his chamber. He doesn't, yet, seem to have any idea what he has done.

But then what *has* he done?

Part III

The Borderline

The question of 'reputation', to the extent that it had ever interested me before this episode, had done so for purely literary, or antiquarian, reasons. It belonged, I assumed, to a bygone world where communications were imperfect and social arrangements consequently more dependent on trust and hearsay than they are now. In the past your 'name' – what other people could report about you – was crucial to your survival, whether you were a medieval knight or an Elizabethan merchant or a Victorian governess. A stain on your honour was potentially catastrophic, and so you guarded it jealously and defended it, if necessary, with your life.

In our own time, with more efficient information systems at our disposal, we were no longer, I supposed, so much at the mercy of other people's perceptions or opinions. Facts could be checked; rumours and falsehoods refuted. A phone or a plane could bring you into direct contact with a potential business partner or employer. Reputation still meant something, but it no longer meant everything, and no longer required the implied threat of pistols at dawn to underwrite it, or suicide to purge its loss. The insane duelling culture of the past – fights to the death over obscure points of musical criticism, demotion to the ranks for failing to resent an insult – had become obsolete and was fast becoming incomprehensible. People could relax, finally, from the state of coiled-up vigilance in which those who wished to get on in the world had spent their lives for so many centuries.

And yet it seems that sometime near the end of the twentieth century, by a curious quirk of scientific progress, history, in this regard, reversed course. The Internet emerged, and with it the arbitration of reality began to pass back from the realm of verifiable fact to that of rumour and report, from the actual to the virtual. The latter, an indiscriminate tumult of truth and lies, was the zone in which our public identities, our outer selves, once again began to assume their definitive form. There was the private self, still, but for anyone who interacted with the world there was this strange new emanation of yourself, your Internet presence, and it was by this, increasingly, that others knew you and judged you.

Very quickly it was discovered that you could manipulate it: glamorise your image, finesse your biography. And by the same token, you could manipulate other people's presences: boost an ally's standing, or launch a corrosive lie against an enemy. One would think that the ease of performing such manipulations, and the large scale on which they immediately began occurring, would have long ago discredited the Web as a source of information about anything, but although we all acknowledge the need to be cautious, to discount much of what we read, split the difference between conflicting statements and so on, our first instinct, being creatures of the Word, is to trust it, and even on deeper consideration we tend to feel that it is basically more right than wrong, and that we can accept its approximations as the truth. You are what the Web says you are, and if it misrepresents you, the feeling of outrage, anguish, of having been violated in some elemental layer of your existence, is, as I began to learn, peculiarly crushing. Reputation ('the gentleman's second soul', as someone put it) is once again asserting its power to make or break us. At the present time of writing, a teenage girl has just hanged herself, a victim of cyber-attacks, and the papers are full of editorials about the deadly effectiveness of this form of bullying, how much more dangerous it is than the old-fashioned kind. I believe it. The essence of bullying is to convey the impression that the bully is the representative of a group, a majority, a consensus, while the victim is all alone. With the Internet the scale of alliances that the oppressor can suggest is limitless, and the feeling of isolation in the victim becomes correspondingly acute. And because, being human, one attributes a kind of human consciousness to this seething electronic data cloud, one also attributes to it a capacity for coherent judgement. The world has decided I am a loser, a monster, a jerk, a slut, whatever, goes the logic of the despairing outcast; how can I ever hope to counteract something so vast, and if I can't, how can I ever show my face again? Spite has never had such an efficient instrument at its disposal.

The Amazon postings came down, but others went up. On a popular book site, Goodreads.com, I found another attack on my story 'The Siege' (here retitled 'Besieged' after a movie based on it). The review was posted by someone calling herself Elise but there was no doubt in my mind that it was Nasreen. Her imitation of the steely tones of scholarly disquiet begins alarmingly well: 'The premise is racist and horribly frightening, considering the reality of surveillance issues in many developing nations . . .' Halfway through there's a slight lapse in verbal poise: 'There is a trend of uppidy perversion in Mr. Lasdun's books, which is creepy though not interesting . . .' I hoped that 'uppidy' might indicate something not quite trustworthy about the attack, but the last sentence resumes control with a masterfully understated little piece of nastiness that left me bathed in cold sweat:

'It's worrisome that he teaches at colleges . . .'

Once again I seemed to be observing my reflection, my 'second soul', undergoing some transformation that I was helpless to prevent. Here I was, a standard-issue liberal with unimpeachably correct views on everything, casting the shadow of some leering, reactionary bigot. Unlike Amazon, Goodreads doesn't have a 'report' option for malicious postings, so there it still sits today, a little inexhaustible font of poison spreading its plumes into the hitherto clear waters of my virtual self.

Some years earlier I'd been given a short entry in Wikipedia. It was full of minor inaccuracies and misrepresentations (it called me an academic, for instance, which I am not). Trivial as these things were, and presumably not malicious, they bothered me much more than they would have done in an old-fashioned printed reference work. There, they would have simply been mistakes: amenable to correction. Here, they seemed to *usurp* the facts. Wikipedia says you are an academic? Very well, you are an academic. I had no idea how to go about altering the entry; as a matter of fact I didn't know it *could* be altered until I got an email from Nasreen with a jeering hint in it about tampering with Wikipedia entries.

The foreboding I experienced as I logged on to Wikipedia.org and checked my entry can be easily imagined. (This cyber-narcissism, not a vice I'd been prone to before, was another gift from Nasreen: I became – it sounds like a malady from some Victorian hygiene pamphlet – a compulsive self-googler.) Was Wikipedia now going to declare me some kind of notorious Zionist literary racketeer? Interestingly, given that she had figured out how to vandalise the site, Nasreen's attack seemed, on the face of it, oddly restrained. There were no accusations of plagiarism, no pseudo-scholarly exposés of misogyny or racism. Instead, there was a single, scatological phrase, inserted into a passage quoting the judges' citation for an award I had won for a story. It was extremely silly, but it had a certain wit, jumping out from the otherwise staid language of a typical Wiki entry, and I might have laughed if the entry hadn't been about me. No doubt, like King Midas whispering to the reeds about his asses' ears, I am doing myself no favours by repeating it, but my interest

112

here is in presenting this case in all its rich awfulness, not in preserving my dignity. 'We chose the story that lingered most,' the judges had written, to which Nasreen had appended: 'like a fart'.

I didn't think much of it at first, but when I checked again a few weeks later and saw that it was still there, lingering malodorously over my entry, I began to sense that it was a cleverer attack than I had realised. Outright denunciations would have aroused suspicion in a Wikipedia entry, which, unlike an Amazon review, is presumably supposed to be neutral. This, however, was like a piece of sly, barely noticeable graffiti that might make people chuckle but probably wouldn't cause them to try to do anything about it, even if they knew how. But its real harm was the notice it gave that I was a person to whom such a thing could be done: that I had attracted an enemy who wanted the world to categorise me as an object of scorn. Whether randomly or out of deliberate selection, I had been successfully targeted, and with the most primevally effective form of malediction: my name mingled with the smell of shit. Cockroaches, vermin, excrement . . . there are certain phenomena that, purely by association, have an ability to reassign a person from the category of human being, in their fellow citizens' minds, to that of waste. All one has to do to trigger the process is find an arresting way of raising the connection. From my self-googling I knew that this Wikipedia entry was usually the first link that came up under my name, which meant that it was the site most commonly visited by anyone looking me up. Again, I am conscious of the dangers of exaggeration here, of sounding self-important or even paranoid (though God knows I did become paranoid in time), and I should say that I realise, again, that probably only a handful of people have ever had any reason to look me up on Wikipedia. But there it was, nevertheless, and it was impossible for me not to imagine the wave of reflexively withdrawn interest, accompanied by the wrinkling of noses, as these people, however few they were, thought better of reading my books, or hiring me to teach, or inviting me to give a reading, or commissioning an article from me, and typed another author's name into the search box instead – someone who didn't trail this unwholesome aura of trouble. I did complain to Wikipedia, and in time received a sympathetic note back, but it was several months before the entry was changed, and by then I had begun to feel like a leper.

Along with these Web attacks, there was yet another development in the email campaign. From my imagined co-conspirators, Nasreen had now progressed to emailing organisations I was professionally associated with. My literary agency in London was sent an email accusing me of the familiar crimes. The Personals department of the *London Review of Books*, bizarrely, was sent an enraged email heaping curses on me (Nasreen obligingly copied me on this). As a freelance writer I depend for my living on easy relations with magazines, newspapers, creative-writing departments, reading venues, and so on. Nowadays any involvement you might have with such places leaves some kind of record on the Web. All Nasreen had to do was work her way through my Google pages and she could systematically denounce me to every one of them. Given her explicit intent to 'ruin' me, I had to assume that this was what she was doing. Very rapidly my relations with all of them became tinged, on my side, with anxiety. Had she contacted them? If so, were they interested? Concerned? Indifferent? I could have asked them, of course, but the thought of doing so seemed, as I considered it, fraught with difficulties. If they hadn't heard from her, what would they make of my strange tale of a former student denouncing me as a plagiarising sexual predator? Somehow it seemed a mistake to introduce such a concept of myself into the minds of other people, even my friends. And if they *had* heard from her, well, what good would it do for me to ask them to please take no notice of what she said? Some of these organisations knew me well enough to dismiss out of hand any of Nasreen's slanders, but some, I had to surmise, might be given pause, if only by that admirable human instinct for fair play. Putting myself in their position, I had no choice (as I imagined them reading her accusations) but to regard myself in a new and questionable light, and it seemed to me I could sense the first small but decisive motions of disengagement. I quickly succumbed to a kind of paralysed dread: fearing the worst on every front, nervously examining my correspondence with these people for signs of distrust, attributing longer than usual silences to decisions to cut me off, but unable to bring myself to find out if the worst had actually occurred.

The culminating act in this particular line of attack came in April 2008. I had taken a teaching job at a college near where I live, to supplement my regular fall job at Morgan College. My boss – I'll call him Frank – was a man in his sixties, an enthusiastic supporter of contemporary writing. There were four other writers in the department and three administrative assistants. Our offices were on the top floor of the campus library. The atmosphere was relaxed, though 'relaxed', by this time, wasn't really a condition I was able to partake in personally.

One morning, shortly after I arrived for work, there was a knock on my door. It was Frank, looking uncharacteristically ill at ease. He had a piece of paper in his hand.

'We've been sent a very weird email,' he said. 'Maybe you should read it.'

I knew immediately what it was. The subject heading ran:

James Lasdun, important information about your "writer-in-residence"

The email itself is rather long, but it seems necessary to reproduce it here in its entirety. I omit only some phrases that might identify other people. X, Y and Z refer, as earlier, to the Iranian writers I was supposed to have helped. I should also mention that the poem I had begun writing on my cross-country train trip the year before had been published by now, under the title 'Bittersweet'. It is fairly obviously about my father (you can google it), but Nasreen had apparently decided it was in fact about her: 'Lasdun,' she had written earlier to someone else, '[. . .] has his "lovers" books reworked. He then writes Bittersweet claiming that I didn't want fame, money etcetera.' Finally, I should stress that, in order for the full impact of this new email to be felt, it must be read as if by my boss himself, who at this point had no inkling of the psychodrama going on in the background of his new hire:

To Whom It May Concern:
I am a former female student of James Lasdun and find it truly disturbing that he is allowed to teach on any level. During my time as his student he did no work on my writing nor on any other female writer's work. He did sleep with the well-connected [Elaine Baker] [. . .] and had an on-going affair, which ended in her harassing and stalking me and sending me disgustingly explicit stories about their relationship when she found out he'd taken me to his agent Janice Schwartz.

It turned out that James Lasdun was not interested in my work but was trying to sleep with me. This, after I'd been raped while trying to finish my work, a novel about pre-revolutionary Iran with an emphasis on the atrocities committed against muslims. His agent sent me to Paula Kurwen, who told me she'd edit my work and to continue working on it while keeping silent and not speaking with any agents or editors (though Schwartz said she would not take on my work). In the meantime, Schwartz, with the aid of her neo-con friends X and Y set out to find two Jewish writers and one Zoroastrian to essentially duplicate my

116

work. And then James Lasdun, after a long email relationship and warnings about him from Ms. Baker, cut me off completely. I never had an affair with him but had developed a psychological bond akin to Stockholm Syndrome.

James Lasdun's poetry is mediocre. His fiction is often racist (I find nothing refreshing about Besieged, a story about an English composer who manipulates a dark woman into fucking him in order to get his help). This is the psychology of your writer-in-residence, at an era when misogyny is no longer romantic.

James Lasdun is probably hard at work writing yet another sadistic tale about me, just like his previous awful, crass poem Bittersweet, knowing that I had dwindled down to 98 pounds after he and his evil witches (Kurwen and banker Schwartz) deceived and stole from me—and after I'd been raped by a colleague at a magazine while writing my book in a 3 month period after finding out that somehow Ms Z was writing the same book (James Lasdun was my advisor on it and apparently he knew, I later found out).

If this is the business side of publishing I would like to vomit on all of you who contribute to such a shallow culture by promoting these people within who are nothing but destructive to beauty, truth and peace.

Please read Coetzee's Diary of a Bad Year. It seems many people are aware of Mr. Lasdun's penchant for daytrading fiction for lack of money and talent. And now you are funding him to exploit me yet again because in my state of trauma and naive trust in him I told him many things, and this is precisely his plan, as he's told me in the last email he sent.

117

I hope all the people involved in this rot in hell. And
I wish these institutions of higher learning would stop
being the banks they are. And I wish you'd keep Mr. Lasdun
away from young women over which he has power. It is the
only way this twisted, sadistic man can get his kicks.
    Best,
    Nasreen

For some time after I had finished reading I was unable to
speak.

Frank seemed as embarrassed as I was. He had stood up and was
pacing up and down my small office.

'Listen,' he said, 'I just want you to know that I don't regard it as
any of my business who you've had affairs with in the past. It's this
other stuff that –'

'But I haven't had an affair,' I said, my voice thick and constricted.

'I don't mean with her, I mean with –' He peered at the email.
'With the other girl – Elaine.'

'I haven't had an affair with *anyone*!' I was agitated, eager to get
the point over.

'All right. Fine. And like I say it's not my concern. But it's this
other stuff that bothers me. These accusations of – I mean what does
this even mean, "daytrading fiction"?'

Of Nasreen's many smears, I had always imagined the sexual
ones would be the most likely to harm me, particularly in the context of my teaching jobs. Hackneyed as it has become, the combi-
nation of elements – male professor, distraught female student,
allegation of impropriety – is still potent. Nasreen was accusing me
of sleeping with another student, not her, but clearly she was presenting this as a form of sexual harassment, and in fact at many colleges it would be considered precisely that (the reasoning is apparently
that if you are sleeping with one student, this might cause you to

118

give lower grades to others). But while it was a relief to find Frank unconcerned about these particular accusations, it was disconcerting to find him stalled by the other ones, which had seemed to me so self-evidently absurd. Not that he was saying he actually believed them, but he clearly felt that some explanation was called for before he could simply dismiss them. No doubt I would have reacted the same way in his position, but even so, the fact that a person of obvious sophistication would feel professionally obliged to give even passing consideration to this fantasy of a gang of neocon word pirates filled me with a crushing sense of the difficulties that lay ahead of me.

But before I describe the rest of this conversation and its aftermath, I must backtrack a little, to a development of my own that I haven't yet mentioned – one that had been progressing for some time.

I imagine that by now anyone reading this document will have at least one fairly pressing question: if I was innocent of everything Nasreen accused me of in her emails to me and other people, then why hadn't I tried to stop them?

The answer is that I had: several times, and in several different ways.

Two or three months into the campaign, I had called the FBI. It had occurred to me that I was the victim of a hate crime, and this, as I understood it, was a federal offence. I can't say I actually felt 'victimised' by Nasreen's anti-Semitism at that point; more just bewildered. But I definitely wanted the emails to stop, and the thought of being in a position to unleash the FBI on Nasreen had filled me with a brief surge of hope.

I spoke to several people, first at the FBI headquarters in New York and then at my local office in Albany. I was listened to patiently. Polite noises of sympathy were made. Off the cuff advice was offered

(I was told on no account to block the emails or stop reading them, in case I missed some overt threat of violence, and not to write back either). But it became obvious, pretty quickly, that nobody was taking the matter as seriously as I was. And I realised, in fact, as I heard myself telling my bizarre story for the third or fourth time, that I probably sounded like a minor sort of lunatic and was just being humoured, no doubt according to strict procedures laid down for dealing with crazy-sounding members of the public. The emails themselves, when I read them over the phone, elicited some grudging interest, but it seemed they weren't threatening enough to warrant intervention from the FBI. For that, I would need direct, repeated death threats and even these would have to be explicitly related to my being Jewish. Nasreen's description of herself as a 'verbal terrorist', which I had looked on as my trump card, produced little more than mildly puzzled indifference. An agent at the Albany office told me to keep him posted if things got worse, but I had the distinct sense (and this may have been an early symptom of my burgeoning paranoia) that he found me ridiculous, possibly even rather contemptible, for trying to turn the big guns of law enforcement against these harmless, if nasty, squibs. A part of me couldn't help agreeing with him. The figure that comes to me – grandiose, but somehow irresistible – is Israel's invasion of Gaza after the cross-border rocket attacks: laser strikes and phosphorous bombs in retaliation for some rusty old Qassams . . . How could that not look awful? And by the same token, how does a middle-aged man, a member of the 'axis of virtue', with all the advantages of his more or less comfortable position in life, fight a young, struggling Iranian woman filled with the sense of her own marginality, without feeling (and looking) like a jerk, a pussy, a chickenhawk imperialist, a 'fucking faggot coward'?

For several weeks I reverted to stoical silence. But then this too started to feel like impotence (the logic of the situation seemed to be that *everything*, on my side, would sooner or later feel like impotence).

As other people were dragged into the affair, efforts at mounting some kind of collective defence began again, and this time they were more concerted. Phone calls were exchanged, strategies discussed, lawyers consulted. Still, it was surprisingly hard to come up with a plan. None of the lawyers seemed sure how to handle the matter, and anyway even the most basic legal action would have been unaffordable. Someone was given the name of a private security company that specialised in stalkers. I called them up and spoke to a man who seemed to be hinting, through careful euphemism, that the key to his company's success lay in threatening to break the stalkers' legs. This didn't seem a very sensible way to go. At one point Paula, who for a period had been getting almost as many emails as I was, took a chance on going against the universal advice not to respond in any way to Nasreen, and wrote her an email (I should mention that I still hadn't met Paula, conspiracies notwithstanding, and that it was through Janice that I heard about this). I saw the email after a document was compiled for the police out of all our correspondence. It was a very compassionate email, gently refuting the accusations, empathising with the various kinds of pain involved in writing a book, and suggesting, among other things, that Nasreen might want to get some counselling. In reply she received a torrent of outstandingly vicious (even by Nasreen's standards) abuse.

When the net of targets spread to include other writers at Morgan College, someone suggested we ask the school itself to help us. This had crossed my mind already, but I'd held back, basically out of embarrassment. Being the focus of a former student's meltdown in which words like 'rape', 'racist', and 'theft' are being tossed around isn't a subject you'd want to raise with your employers at an American writing programme if you didn't absolutely have to. But as other faculty members began receiving emails from Nasreen, so my reticence became pointless, and I began to talk.

The response was surprisingly warm and sympathetic (so much so that I had to wonder whether the repressive forces I had begun to see everywhere in American society might possibly be more a creation of my own anxieties than objective phenomena). Urgent, concerned phone calls and emails were sent out from various offices. I wrote, on request from the dean's office, an account of everything that had happened between me and Nasreen. I distributed copies of Nasreen's emails with annotations explaining the more puzzling references in them. I described my attempts to get the FBI involved in the matter and suggested the administration approach the FBI themselves. They responded that they didn't have legal standing to do so, since the school itself wasn't a target, but instead they proposed sending Nasreen an official 'cease and desist' letter. This sounded promising to me. Being easily intimidated by the law, I tend to assume others will be just as docile. I didn't see the letter itself, but Nasreen copied me on her reply. '**Sue me**,' runs the subject heading of her forwarding email, '**go ahead, call your little lawyers . . .**'

The text contained a threat, of sorts – 'I would probably harm him if I saw him on the street' – which, by the perverse logic of the situation, counted as a nugget of good news (it raised the possibility of criminal prosecution), but otherwise it was just the usual splatter of accusation and invective.

So much for 'ceasing and desisting'. But meanwhile I had had a meeting with the school's head of security, a former cop, who gave me the number of a police detective in the NYPD, I'll call him Detective Bauer, who had experience dealing with this kind of problem.

I phoned the detective at once. He was brisk but courteous, and seemed willing to get involved. We arranged to meet the following week at his precinct building.

I have vivid memories of this meeting. It took place on a sunny morning in the early spring of 2008. As I walked from the subway I could feel a kind of thin, improbable elation flickering inside the otherwise black mood engulfing me. I couldn't quite get over the thought that I was on my way to a meeting with an NYPD detective. My cherished principle of 'internal necessity' seemed to have converged, miraculously, with the principle of action, and here I was taking matters into my own hands: exercising 'agency'.

The station was near my old neighbourhood, and a certain nostalgia further intensified this volatile state of mind. Here was the street where I had lived when I first arrived in New York twenty years ago. Here was our old apartment, K——'s and mine. Here was the street where the woman had called down to me from her window. The sidewalk trees were dotted with tight buds. Banks of tulips in a window box glowed in the sunlight.

Patrol cars and traffic scooters crowded the sidewalk outside the precinct building. Inside, a desk sergeant directed me upstairs to the detectives' office. I climbed a flight of worn steps. A metal door opened onto a large, open, bustling room. Officers, uniformed and plain-clothed, sat at desks that ran the length of it in two rows, interviewing people, talking on the phone, working at laptops. To the left was a barred cell with a bench on which a young man in handcuffs was sitting, head bowed, a uniformed woman leaning against the wall opposite, staring down at him.

Detective Bauer's desk was at the far end of the room. He stood up as I approached and shook my hand. He wore a brown jacket and tie. I suspect he was about my age, though I perceived him as older. He was pinkish and sandy-haired with very light brown eyes, pale-lashed. His face was large, his body heavy-framed.

He pointed to a swivel chair by his desk and I sat down.

Just as we started talking my cell phone rang. It was my daughter, twelve then, and I took the call, excusing myself to the detective, who smiled affably. It wasn't anything important and I got off quickly, explaining to my daughter that I was in New York, talking to a detective about Nasreen

As I hung up it occurred to me that the call had very conveniently solved the problem of how to present myself to the detective as a family man with nothing to hide, something that had
seemed important to establish. But then almost immediately I
began to wonder if it might have seemed a little too perfectly timed,
raising suspicions that I'd set it up in advance, which would of
course have suggested the opposite: a furtive, private, calculating
type . . . Another of Nasreen's legacies: this corrosive tendency to
question and distrust all impressions of other people, my own of
them as well as theirs of me.

'So this lady,' the detective resumed. 'Remind me. She's a student
of yours?'

'She was, several years ago. It's a complicated story.'

As succinctly as I could, and uncomfortably aware of all the
other people in the room, I told the detective the story of my ac-
quaintance with Nasreen: her term as my student, the friendly correspondence we'd had when she got back in touch two years later,
the outburst when I made it clear I wasn't interested in having an
affair, the resumption of our amicable correspondence, my gradual
backing away as she started forwarding other people's emails and
deluging me with her own, the hate mail, accusations and strange
demands for my apartment keys that began after this withdrawal
became complete. I did my best to supply the logic linking this chain
of events, though I was aware of its sounding pretty tenuous, almost
as if I had come there to complain about a bad dream I'd had. And I
made sure the detective understood that although I was the main
target of Nasreen's wrath, other people, principally Janice and Paula,
had been sent equally venomous emails. I didn't want him to con-
clude this was all just some murky tale of an illicit affair gone sour,
as I imagined I might have done in his position.

He listened without interrupting and nodded thoughtfully when
I had finished. If the world of graduate writing programmes, literary

agents, freelance editors, publishing deals, intellectual property and so on was at all mysterious to him, he didn't show it. His demeanour was calm, a little detached but sympathetic, like that of a physician one is consulting for the first time and filling in on the intimate history of one's ailments.

He asked if I'd brought the emails, and I handed him a selection I'd made from each of the different phases I'd described. He looked through them in silence, taking his time. On a cabinet behind him was a fish tank. The fish in it appeared to be tiny sharks: black with white underbellies, triangular dorsal fins and pugnacious, wedge-shaped heads. I'd never seen anything like them and wondered if they were a standard feature of detectives' rooms, or peculiar to this precinct. Not that there was anything sharkish, on the face of it, about Detective Bauer. If anything he seemed a rather mild man. He appeared to be genuinely shocked by Nasreen's emails. His pinkish complexion was mottled with darker reds as he looked up from them.

'All this stuff about drugs,' he said, frowning. 'I don't like that.'

That took me by surprise. Nasreen often mentioned smoking pot or taking speed, but I'd never given it much thought. To the detective, however, these casual references to an illegal activity were apparently not something to be glossed over so easily. I had the feeling he was almost personally affronted by them, and I felt a bit embarrassed at having revealed my lack of concern about them.

I nodded lamely. 'What about the other stuff?'

'Well, it's aggravated harassment, no question. We'd pick her up right now if she was in New York. But you're saying she moved to California?'

'According to her.'

'That could be a problem.'

Aggravated harassment, he explained, was a misdemeanour rather than a felony, and it was unlikely, given the expense involved, that a district attorney was going to have her extradited from California to New York just for a misdemeanour.

'I'll talk to the DA's office, I'll definitely do that, but even with something as bad as this' – he motioned with what seemed to be sincere disgust at the pile of emails –'it's going to be a long shot.'

But he had another proposition. In his experience, he said, a call from an NYPD detective was usually enough to stop this kind of thing. He would call up Nasreen and talk to her, tell her that if she continued harassing me or any of her other targets in any way, which meant any kind of contact at all, she'd be arrested and brought to New York to face charges.

'It's a little bit of a bluff, since like I say the DA probably isn't going to want to spend the money to have her extradited, but with luck she'll take me at my word. They usually do.'

Though I didn't want to discourage him, I thought I should tell him how she'd responded to the cease and desist letter from Morgan College. He nodded, but didn't seem too concerned.

'We'll see what happens. Another thing we can do if this doesn't work is arrange to have a couple of officers out in California drop in on her. That can sometimes get a result.'

I said I thought that would be an excellent idea. There was a pause.

'What do you think of her?' I asked. 'I mean, what do you think's actually going on?'

He looked away a moment, then looked back.

'I have relatives with a daughter like her,' he said. 'Same kind of what you'd call borderline personality. Sometimes she'll do stuff like this and her parents'll call me. I've had to deal with her multiple times.'

'Borderline? You mean as in . . . on the edge, psychologically?'

He shrugged.

'Able to act very crazy if they want to but also able to control it if they want to.'

The subject had brought a look of melancholy sympathy to his features. He was an odd mixture of compassion and rather old-fashioned severity.

I'd wanted to ask him more about his understanding of 'border-line personalities', but the meeting was apparently over.

'So anyway,' he said, standing up, 'give me a little time, but I'll definitely call her, and we'll take it from there. OK?'

I nodded, thanking him effusively.

Nasreen had sent me various phone numbers over the years, including those of family members out in California (she'd copied me, God knows why, on her correspondence with some of them), and I gave these to Detective Bauer.

I left feeling cautiously optimistic.

This, more or less, was where matters stood when Frank appeared at my door with Nasreen's email denouncing me as a racist, a thief, a mediocre writer and a danger to young women.

I had spoken once more to Detective Bauer by then, to report a new development in the emails, a disturbing one (but all developments in this saga were disturbing), and to see if he'd spoken to Nasreen yet. He hadn't, though he assured me he would soon and asked me to fax him the new emails. But just the fact that I had reported the matter to him, that it was now an official police matter, proved extremely helpful. As I began trying to explain to Frank that every one of Nasreen's assertions was a lie, I had felt that, although he personally believed me, in his professional capacity he needed something stronger than just my word against Nasreen's. At any rate, as soon as I told him about my meeting with Detective Bauer, he looked immensely relieved, and by the end of our conversation he was offering his full support and sympathy. At my urging he called

Morgan College to verify what I'd told him and coordinate a response. Soon after that his own administration contacted their local police on my behalf, who opened their own file on Nasreen.

In practical terms then, I was unharmed by this latest strike. But by that stage I was in more danger from the psychological effects of Nasreen's campaign than from any practical damage she may have inflicted.

She had been sending me hate email now for almost a year. On the advice of police, lawyers and friends, I'd refrained from blocking it, not that this would have been easy to do anyway, as she continually set up new email addresses. As she explained, with her usual candour: 'I keep changing my email address because I think you are blocking and silencing me and punishing me for my pain.' Sometimes, when I couldn't face reading the messages, I saved them without opening them. And sometimes, especially when I came on a whole clutch of fresh arrivals gleaming malevolently in my inbox, I deleted them without opening them, dispatching them in a brief frenzy of defiance, though I always regretted this later (what if I had just deleted the one unequivocal threat that would have elevated her crime to a felony and triggered extradition?). For a period, when I was close to the borderline myself, I asked K— to check my email before I looked, and to save anything from Nasreen without telling me about it unless it contained a radical new development: I needed to be able to tell myself that the attacks *might* be coming to an end. But mostly I read them, and it was like swallowing a cup of poison every morning, with usually a few more cupfuls to follow later in the day.

If her aim, as a verbal terrorist, was to replicate the conditions of the nation at large inside my head, with its panics and paranoias, its thrashing impotence, its schizoid shame and self-righteousness, its droning monomania, she succeeded triumphantly. Possibly the monomania, the increasing difficulty of thinking about anything other than Nasreen, was the worst of these effects. In this respect her obsession with me achieved perfect symmetry: I became just as obsessed with her. I couldn't write, read, play with my kids, listen to the news, do almost anything, without drifting off, for longer and longer intervals, into morbid speculations about what new mischief she might be getting up to. The sheer quantity of her emails was such that I never had time to recover my equilibrium between them. Even the ones that just consisted of abuse left a bruised, unclean feeling, and there was never time to purge this, so that an accumulation of unprocessed disgust, pain and bewilderment seemed to be piling up inside me. I lived, increasingly, in the medium of Nasreen's hatred. I couldn't think about anything except her, and pretty soon I couldn't *talk* about anything except her.

This meant that in situations where I didn't feel comfortable raising the subject, I would fall into heavy, unsociable silence, while in situations where I did feel comfortable, I would talk about nothing else. Up to a point, people found it interesting. Some responded with stalker stories of their own. A writer friend who had judged a literary competition was being plagued with abuse by one of the entrants, accusing her of stealing his material. A therapist I knew was being sued by a former patient whom she had helped find a job that hadn't worked out. A couple of male acquaintances confided that they were being harassed by women they'd had one-night stands with. All moderately comforting, though since none of it was on anything like the scale of Nasreen's campaign, it left me feeling, more than ever, the sheer singularity of my case, which in turn reinforced the sense of its insolubility. Besides, as I heard myself droning on compulsively to these friends and acquaintances, I could feel, among even the most patient and sympathetic, a certain resistance building: not boredom exactly (the continually evolving weirdness of the story seemed to ensure, if nothing else, a degree of fascination); more a kind of helplessness. What could they do, finally, about this intractable problem of mine? And when there is nothing you can do about a person's suffering, there comes a point where you don't want to hear about it any more.

Depression, anxiety, insomnia . . . one by one the symptoms of stress took over my life. Irritability too. I don't usually get angry easily, but at home I became short-tempered, and even out in public I was uncharacteristically prickly. Once, in an espresso bar around the corner from our apartment, I almost attacked a man. It was a tiny place with just a few small tables that patrons were expected to clear off themselves when they were finished. I was standing with my cup of coffee, waiting for a table, when the man and his girlfriend got up to leave without observing this basic courtesy. They were English, so, fair enough, there was no reason why they should have known it was the custom. Very politely I asked them if they were leaving.

'Yes.'

'Would you mind throwing out your stuff?'

The man, about my age, looked peeved, but said OK.

'You can just put it there, in the garbage,' I told him, still perfectly polite.

The man threw out his paper plates and napkins. Then he looked directly at me with a nasty smile and said:

'*Sieg Heil.*'

Under normal circumstances I'd have been too dumbstruck, and too inhibited about making a scene in public, to come up with any kind of retort until long after such an incident was over. But I was in such a coiled-up state of tension by that point that I reacted without hesitation:

'What?' I said quietly.

He continued smiling. I took a step towards him.

'Do you want me to throw a cup of boiling coffee in your face?'

His smile turned a bit sickly: 'All right, I just –'

'You must be out of your fucking mind, saying something like that to a Jew in New York.'

'I . . . I'm sorry.'

'People clear their stuff away here. There aren't any waiters.'

He swallowed, then pouted: 'Well . . . I don't like being told what to do.'

At this point I became louder. 'I wasn't fucking telling you what to do. I was just asking you to get your fucking crap off the table.'

At that he moved towards the exit. 'OK, I . . . I apologise. I apologise.'

As he and his girlfriend left, I became aware that everyone in the tiny cafe was looking at me in silence. Perhaps no one else had heard his *'Sieg Heil'* or, if they had, had known what to make of it (it's a peculiarly English put-down, and an antiquated one at that). Far from applauding me or even nodding mild approval, they were looking at me as if I might be about to take out a gun and start shooting. I left, feeling distinctly that I wasn't going to be welcome back there.

And then there was the paranoia. This manifested itself in a number of ways, but the source, the underlying premise of them all, lay in Nasreen's uncanny ability to orchestrate other people, or at least the illusion of other people, into her attacks. Paranoia is a dysfunction in one's relations with other people. It requires a social context, and Nasreen's incorporation of my various personal and professional associates into her campaign supplied this very efficiently. It also requires a constantly shifting boundary between what one knows for a fact and what one can only imagine, and this too, this destabilising principle, was supplied by Nasreen. All she had had to do was introduce the concept of smearing my name, and furnish a few concrete examples of having done so, and my anxious self-interest could be relied on to expand the process indefinitely. The calculus was simple: if a person is prepared to falsely assert X about you, then why would she not also falsely assert Y? Why, in fact, would she not assert every terrible thing under the sun? And if that person has already demonstrably reported those terrible things to your agent, your boss, your colleagues, then why might she not also be in the process of reporting them to your neighbours, your friends, your editor at this or that paper or magazine, your relatives, et cetera?

I fell prey to the worst imaginings; suspecting, increasingly, that everyone I spoke to on the phone or ran into in town had heard Nasreen's allegations about me, either directly from Nasreen or in the form of rumours set off by some Web posting of hers, and that they were secretly harbouring the thought that the soft-spoken Englishman in their midst might be some kind of monster. The fact that I had written a novel, *The Horned Man*, in which a college instructor believes he is being framed for a series of sex crimes, gave the situation a piquancy that didn't escape me, though I was in no condition to enjoy it ('How I had managed to lay myself open to an act of such preposterously elaborate vindictiveness,' my hero reflects with a pertinence I struggle to find purely coincidental, 'how or why such an intricate engine of destruction could ever have docked at *my* life, was still unfathomable . . .'). On rare occasions when I was able to persuade myself that this really *was* all a case of my own worst imaginings, Nasreen would invariably deliver some dismaying new evidence to the contrary. I remember at one point wondering if my sudden interest in honour, name, 'reputation' was a bit fanciful, a case of allowing writerly interests to shape the way I was experiencing this ordeal. But in February 2008 a volley of emails arrived in which Nasreen explicitly targets these entities, plucking the words, it seemed, straight out of my own mind. '**Your reputation is ass . . .**' runs the inimitably phrased heading of the first email in this volley. 'You think you're clever but your name is tarnished,' goes a line in the next. Just as she had once felt controlled by my fictions ('i'm living your short story out and I'm scared'), so I now began to feel controlled by hers. Never mind that my real self was innocent of everything she accused me of: out there in cyberspace a larger, more vivid version of myself had been engendered and was rapidly (so I felt) supplanting me in the minds of other people: Nasreen's version, the thief, the racist, the sexual predator.

The sexual slander was of course the most dangerous, threatening not just my livelihood but the basic conditions of my life. We know how vulnerable men have become to this taint (women too, though less so). I had observed it repeatedly since moving to the States, from the 'recovered memory' hysteria of the eighties, with its scenes of sheriffs dragging bewildered old fathers off to jail, to the more complex sexual harassment dramas of the nineties. Like most men my age, old enough to have observed the patriarchal model of male behaviour up close and young enough to have recognised its obsolescence, I was in favour of the attempt to regulate it out of existence. But I had seen how easy it was to abuse the shaming and ostracising power the new attitudes brought. At a certain point in the ascendancy of a new idea, just a word can turn a human being into shit: different words in different eras; race words and class words in the past, now sex words.

For some time Nasreen had been very obviously trying to find a way of using this kind of verbal napalm against me. In particular she seemed to have been looking for a formula that would square her acknowledgement that she and I had never come close to any kind of sexual contact, with a paradoxical eagerness to call me a rapist. Already she had found ways of associating me with the idea of rape without actually accusing me of it, but I had sensed that she was moving towards something more direct.

The rape she refers to, so far as I can piece the story together from the various fragmentary accounts she gives in her emails, occurred at the offices of a well-known national magazine where she was working sometime before she enrolled at Morgan College (in other words, sometime before I met her). She had passed out or been drugged at an office event and woken up certain that she'd been assaulted. She had reported it to the police but they had declined to investigate.

Her Amazon review and email to my boss linked me – rhetorically if not factually – with this rape ("It turned out that James Lasdun was not interested in my work but was trying to sleep with me. This, after I'd been raped while trying to finish my work . . .').

But even before this, she had begun to work me into the rape itself, writing in January: 'It's clear James has been using me . . . he may have even initiated the rape so as to steal my work and give it to X . . .' and in February floating the suspicion that I might have been the actual assailant: 'I hope to God James is not my rapist . . .' The practicalities of this scenario, in which my plot against her turns out to have been in motion even before I became her teacher, obliged her to construct a complicated set of motives and connections linking me to her, which in turn required me to have been already working in concert with one of my future colleagues at Morgan College (I'll call her Liz): 'i think he and liz set up my rape . . .'

No doubt these allegations sound too obviously ridiculous or crazed to convince anyone of anything, and perhaps they were. But I don't think Nasreen particularly cared about convincing people. The point, as she had candidly stated, was simply to tarnish and smear – to render me, shall we say, unfit for public consumption. Given the energy she was putting into this, it seemed to me that she was bound to succeed, if not by reason or subtlety then by sheer force of attrition. In the deepening gloom of that winter I began to feel that I and other men were beginning to occupy a position in our society like that of women in repressive traditional societies, where the merest suggestion of sexual transgression could mean death. Like them our reputations were frail, in need of vigilant protection. We needed our own form of purdah, it seemed to me; our own yash-maks and chadors . . . Certainly I could have used something like that after my conversation with Frank. Formally speaking, I was in the clear, my word accepted over Nasreen's, but the nature of a smear is that it survives formal cleansing, and I felt the foulness it had left behind, like an almost physical residue. What did the other people in the department who had read the email think, now, as I passed through the offices? What did these assistants and other teachers see when they looked at me? People die of curses in primitive societies. The victim internalises his designation as poison, excrement, untouchable filth; feels or imagines the community cutting itself off from him and collapses inward. Fatwa, voodoo, excommunication – all attempt to tap into this power, and Nasreen seemed to have found her own way of using it. It became an agony to walk through those grey-carpeted rooms and corridors. I felt the literal reality of that elemental attribute of shame, the desire to hide one's face, and I would have gladly covered mine if some convention for doing so had existed. Somehow I had recreated in my own psyche the America of the Scarlet Letter and the Long Black Veil.

By June 2008 the rhetoric of the emails had reached a logical extreme. Not death threats exactly (Nasreen seems to have been too canny for that); more like death wishes, death prophecies, death curses:

```
I hope he dies if he is behind all this . . .

die. i hope your kids die . . .

Die traitor-ugly-bitches . . . DIE . . .
```

I didn't seriously think she was going to come and kill me, though I did find myself looking closely at the cars that drove by on the dirt road outside our house, and sometimes at night if I heard a sound I would lie half awake for long stretches, wishing I owned a gun. But by this point I was no longer responding so much to the literal content of the emails as to the mere fact of their undiminishing volume and persistence. They reached me less as specific threats than as a kind of pure, abstract antagonism, and I reacted with a correspondingly abstract distillation of pure pain. 'Thinking' about the emails no longer consisted of appraising or trying to understand them, so much as merely feeling them pulsate in my mind like some malignant bolus.

In my initial plan for this part of the story, I had considered transposing an event from fifteen years earlier in my life, in which a prolonged period of stress had culminated in a rather spectacular medical drama. I was afraid all this talk of torment might become a bit vaporous without some concrete dramatic representation to anchor it in reality, and this event would have fitted the bill perfectly.

I had been sitting on my bed when I felt an excruciating pain across my back and left shoulder. I thought I'd pulled a muscle and maybe pinched a few nerves. There was a strange pressure against my lung when I breathed in, and soon I found I couldn't draw in enough breath to fill my lungs. I took some ibuprofen and lay down, trying to rest, but every time I changed my position something seemed to shift inside my chest like a sac filled with oil and gravel, the gravel grinding over a network of nerves as it slowly repositioned itself in the thick oil. Finally I called my doctor, who told me to come in immediately. He listened to my chest and sent me straight to the hospital, where an X-ray revealed that my left lung had collapsed. The emergency-room doctor made an incision over my upper ribcage. Lifting a sharpened steel rod with both hands, he plunged it down between two of my ribs. As I shouted with pain, he stuck a tube into the hole, connected to a device that looked like a small humidifier. Bubbles went up through the water in this, indicating, so he told me, that the lung was reinflating itself.

The condition, known as spontaneous pneumothorax, isn't fully understood, though it has a relatively high rate of incidence among Jewish males in their thirties. I had had TB in my twenties, which the doctor thought might have made me more susceptible. Also, under the stress of the foregoing months I had stupidly started smoking, and this too may have been a factor. But whatever the immediate medical or genetic cause, the occurrence was so irresistibly symbolic of my inability to shake off the burdened feeling that had been afflicting me that I chose to think of it as entirely psychosomatic in origin. Basically I had imploded.

My idea, as I say, had been to move this event into the present narrative, using it to indicate the level of stress I was experiencing under Nasreen's onslaught. But soon after I began writing I realised this strange narrative could work only if I kept very strictly to the facts. So I am obliged to relinquish the scene. But there are other things I could offer in its place that, if less dramatic, were at least a part of the imagery that presented itself to me at the time. Reading Tintin to my son, for instance, *The Seven Crystal Balls* and *Prisoners of the Sun*, I saw myself graphically portrayed in the tomb-robbing Western scientists who fall into comas on returning from South America, and go into paroxysms of pain every few hours as their Inca tormentors back in the Andes stick pins into their doll-like effigies. Those were me, those white, middle-aged men writhing in agony on their beds from some unseen cause. And Rascar Capac, the Inca succubus who breaks into their homes to administer the coma-inducing narcotic; Rascar Capac with his fiendish yet sympathetic presence (after all, he is the avenger of the colonised, the oppressed, the pillaged), his angry dark skull-face and skeletal arms, his affinity with fireballs and lightning and smashed glass; Rascar Capac, 'he-who-unleashes-the-fire-of-heaven', was Nasreen.

She had brought me forcibly into the realm of magical thinking, which is to say she had found a way, whether by luck or intelligence, to inflict pain on me from a distance (or, as K—— corrected me, to cause me to inflict pain on myself) and to sap, steadily, my sense of personal autonomy. The insubstantial nature of her attacks, wafted at me over the ether, was further conducive to the thought of sorcerous powers. I spent less time thinking about lawyers and police (Detective Bauer was proving elusive, though he had repeated his promise to call Nasreen), more about spells and curses. Continually on my mind at this time were the witches' lines from *Macbeth*, where they plot the torment of a hapless ship's captain:

> I will drain him dry as hay:
> Sleep shall neither night nor day
> Hang upon his penthouse lid;
> He shall live a man forbid.
> Weary sev'n-nights nine times nine,
> Shall he dwindle, peak and pine . . .

Those were my symptoms precisely: the insomnia, the dwindling, the peaking and pining. But it was the next two lines, the summation of the *limits* of witchcraft, its power to disturb but not actually capsize one's ship ('bark'), that I clung to as I began to feel myself toppling into the abyss:

> Though his bark cannot be lost,
> Yet it shall be tempest-tost.

This was my charm against despair, and I invoked it over and over, telling myself that although I could be 'tempest-tost' by Nasreen's malice, nothing she had done, not even the email to Frank, had caused me actual objective harm, and, if Shakespeare's formula was applicable to her, nothing could. She might, as K—— had observed, cause me to harm myself, but that was my responsibility, and it was within my power to resist it. All I needed to do was keep a level head. Macbeth allows the witches' prophecies to insinuate themselves, fatally, into his own ambitions and anxieties. But Banquo, who has ambitions of his own and might have been equally thrown by what the witches told him, sees things for what they are: 'oftentimes, to win us to our harm, / The instruments of Darkness tell us truths; / Win us with honest trifles, to betray 's / In deepest consequence . . .' I would be like Banquo, I resolved (passing over the fact that his sceptical rationalism gets him hacked to death a few scenes later); I would take the emails for what they were: sad and pathetic bits of nonsense; barbed, certainly, with their own clever tricks and 'honest trifles', but incapable of causing harm in themselves. I tried to ignore the anxiety that gripped me every time I signed on in the morning; the palpitations in my heart if there was something new from Nasreen in my inbox. But it was difficult. My total failure, after all these months, to slow down or in any way inhibit the flow of hatred had had a demoralising effect (as I write, the BP oil catastrophe is unfolding and it is impossible not to picture Nasreen's hostility as that blackness on the spillcams, billowing unstoppably from the ocean floor, my efforts to staunch it as ineffective as BP's with their feeble funnels and top kills). I felt flayed, utterly defenceless. Every email sent lacerating spasms through me as it struck, each with an afterburn, a half-life, that was nowhere near over before the next one came in, so that I could never regroup my own forces. And meanwhile the hatred itself was achieving ever more potent intensities of compression. A strange new verbal economy seemed to be emerging, a kind of crystalline purity of malediction, as if Nasreen were no longer speaking the language of humans but of demons:

you are hanging yourself with bittersweet. You are fat, old, a thief—and the ones who matter know about you if I could see you, I'd shit in your fat mouth . . .

If you live in fear say it. And say it loud, don't cower
in fucking fear like you did during the holocaust . . .

old, shitty man! two faced psychotic . . .

ha ha ha ha ha ha . . . go to hell, old man . . .

One morning in 2008 I received an email purporting to be from the programme director at Morgan College. He appeared to be forwarding me an article about the Iranian leader Mahmoud Ahmadinejad, and he had accompanied the article with a personal message, though it wasn't written in his usual style:

Let's suck cock together! eat your ugly bittersweet and
die!

I mentioned earlier that sometime after my meeting with Detective Bauer, I had called the detective to report a new development in Nasreen's attacks. This email was its first manifestation.

When you forward an article from a newspaper or magazine website, you generally fill out a form that asks for your own email address as well as that of the recipient, and offers you a space to write a personal message. Well, it turns out that in the space for your own email address you can type in the email address of anyone you want and the article and message will be sent as if from that person. Recently I've noticed that some forwarded articles warn the recipient that the sender's identity hasn't been verified, but this wasn't the case in 2008 and even now it seems to be the exception. Basically, as

Nasreen had discovered, you can pretend to be anyone you want when you forward an article, and she had decided to pretend to be my boss.

As I wrote earlier, I had been struck from the beginning by a certain porousness about Nasreen, a capacity for absorbing other selves or dissolving into them. Her identification with the Angel in Rilke's *Duino Elegies* had led me to Heidegger's essay in which he refers to this Angel as one *for whom borderlines and differences . . . hardly exist any longer.* The connection this remark had suggested, between Nasreen's blurring propensity and the concept of a 'borderline' personality, was cemented (in my mind at least) by Detective Bauer's use of the word 'borderline' to describe his relative, who resembled Nasreen. Amorphousness was Nasreen's element. And if the Internet in general, with its rich opportunities for shape-shifting and self-reinvention, was her natural medium of expression, then this forwarding system was the perfect refinement, allowing her to take on the identity of anyone she liked.

Viewed dispassionately, the phase of attacks that now began has something of the exuberance one sees in artists when their imaginations are seized by some new subject or method, and in a burst of creativity they start delightedly revolving and reconsidering it from every conceivable angle. I imagine that as I describe these emails, some readers will find it hard to suppress a smile, whatever else they may feel. There is always something appealing about the stirrer, the situationist, the inventive mischief-maker.

From 'Elaine', the former classmate with whom Nasreen believed I had had an affair, I received a forwarding about Rwanda with this message attached:

    hi. I'm dumb, stupid and stupid looking and claim to care
    about people. I like to #### old men.

From 'Paula', I got a link to a news story about the Middle East, presumably concerning some action by the Israelis (I didn't open the link), with the message:

```
Don't you think we should just cut it out already?
```

From 'Liz', the colleague at Morgan College with whom I am supposed to have 'set up' Nasreen's rape, I received a story about the Miss Universe Pageant with the message:

```
Look, I got breast implants!
```

And so on. All pretty childish and, in themselves, harmless. But again, it wasn't so much the content that disturbed me as the implied threat of the form: the new field of potential trouble it opened up. How serious was this trick of impersonation going to become? What were its limits and potentialities? It didn't take me long to conjecture that if she was masquerading as other people to me, then she was probably masquerading as *me* to other people. Having already denounced me to every person or institution she could find an email address for, was she now going to confirm her slanders with creepy emails purporting to come directly from me? Visions of articles being forwarded in my name to people I knew, from 'my' email address, with obscene personal messages from me attached, filled my imagination. The situation seemed freshly intolerable. Actually, the sheer unbearableness of it filled me with a brief, paradoxical hope. I remember wondering if it really was possible that Nasreen, even Nasreen, would do something as fiendish as this.

It was, and she did.

Again, there is the swift progression from clumsy first pass to fully evolved weapon. First, before using my email address, Nasreen gets the idea of speaking 'as me' in a faked exchange with Janice.

142

The exchange is set up to look as though Janice is replying to a forwarding from me (about the Armenian genocide). As Janice, Nasreen writes:

> James, please stop sending me notes like the one below.

And as me, in the note below, she writes:

> Janice, I thought we copyrighted all genocides so we can
> nation-build and kill everyone so we can die on the
> mount! Why wouldn't that Iranian bitch fuck me and why is
> she telling the whole world that I fuck any blonde thing
> to overcome my self-hatred?

Next, she starts using my email address, masquerading outright as
me. I don't know how often she did this, but from time to time, presumably just to make sure I wasn't spared any possible nuance of
discomfort, she would copy me on them: the usual garbage, to the
usual recipients, plus some new ones. Here I am, for instance, sending Janice and Paula a story about Swiss banks funding terrorism:

> We will own the middle east before the world ends!

The one consoling thought arising from this new development
was that it presumably constituted some kind of identity theft, which
I hoped might be a serious-enough crime to trigger extradition. I
called Detective Bauer. He asked me to fax him the emails along
with printouts of each 'sender path' – the list of codes you can display
by clicking on 'details' at the top of an email, which identify the actual, precise origin of the email and which, unlike the apparent
sender address, cannot be faked. He agreed that this amounted to
identity theft, but warned me that the Manhattan DA's office had

recently lost a large electronic identity theft case and as a result wasn't currently prosecuting the crime very enthusiastically. Still, he seemed to think these emails put us in a stronger position for dealing with Nasreen. I asked him if he had had a chance to call her yet. He hadn't, but he assured me that he was planning to very soon. Why not right now? I wanted to ask him, but for all his courteous affability, he didn't seem the kind of man you could hurry. He had his own calm, imperturbable pace.

Sometimes I was the recipient as well as the sender of these forwardings, which put me in the disconcerting position of sending obscenities and threats to myself. I felt as if some strange circle of madness was closing. Nasreen herself, in her uncanny way, seems to have intuited as much – perhaps even planned it. As she put it while pretending to be Paula forwarding me a Craigslist posting:

```
The voices in my head told me the voices in your head
might lead us to meet on craigslist . . .
```

But the next major step was much more alarming, if less surreal: online exchanges with the wider world, in my name. I first got wind of this when a secretary from Morgan College called to tell me that a sales rep from Hummer had been trying to set up a meeting with me in response to my email enquiry about buying a vehicle. Aside from the mild embarrassment of being thought of as a would-be Hummer owner by the personnel of Morgan College, there was the depressing thought of having to contend with the sales reps of all the other companies Nasreen had contacted in my name, because, knowing her, there would most certainly be others. There were. For months I was deluged with sales info from companies thanking me for my interest in purchasing their products. Again, relatively trivial irritants in themselves, but as effective as anything else in preserving the sense of being under siege by an indefatigable enemy, and fuel, again, for further anxious speculation as to how matters were going to evolve.

The answer to the latter came in June 2008. I had succumbed to one of my periodic fits of self-googling when I found myself being directed to a Jewish literary site called Nextbook.com. There, in the '**comments**' section, under a review of a first novel, I found the following:

```
I'd like to steal that book to feed my family. I do that
with the help of my agent and heavily connected old bag
friend Paula Kurwen. Don't you know that art is dead and
Israel is great?
Posted by James Lasdun on 06.21.08
```

I emailed a complaint to the site and after a while the posting was taken down, but at this point I began to wonder if the game wasn't as good as over. This other version of me, so much more vital and substantial than I felt myself to be by this time, had completed its usurpation of my identity and was running amok. '**I will not let you go**' went the heading of one of Nasreen's emails from this period, and it confirmed my sense that what was happening could no longer be regarded as a passing unpleasantness, but was a permanent condition.

I called Detective Bauer again. To my surprise, he had initiated contact with Nasreen. He hadn't actually spoken to her, but he had left messages at the numbers I'd given him. He seemed confident that she would return the calls.

I was encouraged by this, but I was apprehensive too. It would have been one thing for Detective Bauer to catch Nasreen off her guard: unprepared for a conversation with a police officer about her emails and therefore more likely to believe him when he threatened her with arrest. But now, with his messages, he'd lost the element of surprise and given her an opportunity not only to prepare her own defence, but also to counter-attack. There was no guessing what new smear or accusation she could possibly invent at this stage, but I imagined there would be something.

All this time I was trying to preserve some semblance of functionality in the other parts of my life. There was the editing of our Provence book to deal with. There were the details of our ignominious 'surrender' agreement on the apartment to finalise. There was my vegetable garden to keep up and a clan of obstinately ingenious groundhogs to keep out.

In some activities I could hold the thought of Nasreen at bay more easily than in others, or at least I was less disabled by it. But as the months passed it seemed to determine the way I experienced just about everything I did. Her inexplicable fixation on our apartment, for instance, seemed to converge with the owner's efforts to drive us out, to the point where her physical appearance began to substitute itself in my mind for that of the owner, whom I had never seen. Likewise with the groundhogs. Defiantly present in my garden every morning despite the skirting of galvanised mesh I'd buried to a depth of two feet underground and the barbed-wire coils I attached to the fence, these creatures became the embodiment of the successive waves of new malice Nasreen kept coming up with. Or they were the emails themselves, sitting in my inbox with that same air of triumphant cunning . . .

The further her occupation of my mind extended, the harder it was to concentrate on anything else. Reading became problematic. Books that required any active effort of engagement were out of the question. At the same time, books that required only passive submission to a well-oiled mechanism of suspense became addictive. Mysteries, crime novels, psychological thrillers were all I read that year. The genres of Ahriman, you could say: narratives of disintegration and ruin, of what Robert Lowell called 'the downward glide and bias of existing', the reading of which was itself a mimicry of the processes of collapse they dramatised. The very opposite of D. H. Lawrence and George Eliot and Tolstoy and all the other life-affirming, upward-aspiring writers whose books at one time had been the only literary company I cared to keep.

Often in these suspense novels I would find echoes of my own predicament: similar structures of anguish; events that strikingly resembled those in my own drama; sometimes entire plotlines. One book in particular seemed to articulate my circumstances during this phase with the same dreamlike, redistributive accuracy as *Gawain* had in that earlier phase. This was Patricia Highsmith's *Strangers on a Train*. I had seen the Hitchcock film but never read the book until now. The train in question turns out to be on its way, as mine had been, to Santa Fe. As evening falls, Guy Haines, a high-minded young man, sits in his Pullman trying to read Plato. He is distracted, however, by anxieties concerning his impending meeting with his estranged wife, Miriam, a manipulative, unfaithful woman from whom he is hoping to obtain a divorce so that he can marry his true soulmate, the lovely Anne. His career is at stake as well as his personal happiness. He is an aspiring architect (a hybrid, you could say, of me and my father) with a high sense of the nobility of this profession, in which the virtuousness of the socially committed intellectual is combined with the prestige of the artist. His prospects are bright on both fronts, home and career, but for the sake of both he needs to purge from his life the error of judgement represented by the tawdry, tacky Miriam. Miriam had agreed to the divorce, but from her last communication Guy has reason to be worried that she isn't, after all, going to let him go.

As he broods on this, while still trying to read his Plato, a young man sits down opposite him. He has an 'interesting face', Guy notices, his skin 'smooth as a girl's'. There is something seedy about him, though also something beguilingly open and friendly. This is Charles Anthony Bruno, the first of Highsmith's great studies in the psychopathic mind. He smiles at Guy, who at once retreats into his book. A moment later, however, racked by a renewed spasm of anxiety over Miriam, Guy accidentally touches Bruno's outstretched foot with his own.

In D. H. Lawrence, accidental physical contact of this kind will often (as in the story 'You Touched Me') provide the spark that awakens lovers to their transfiguring passions for each other. In Highsmith, the touch sets off a similarly intense involvement, but of a deathward orientation, its eroticism purely disintegrative, like the hectic colours of fall.

The two start talking: Guy reservedly at first, Bruno with a gushing candour that disarms Guy and fascinates him despite the dubious things Bruno reveals about himself, the most notable of which is an obsessive resentment of his father, whom he would very much like to kill.

Full of self-deprecating charm, he persuades Guy to dine with him in his roomette (though the word doesn't appear to have entered the Amtrak lexicon yet), where, as they get drunk together, he begins questioning Guy about his private life. In no time he has wheedled the whole story of Miriam out of Guy and begun insinuatingly probing into Guy's feelings about her infidelities, the other men, the possible hold-up of the divorce, subtly but firmly bringing to the surface of Guy's mind all his suppressed rage and hatred. What he is after is an admission that Guy would like to kill Miriam, just as he, Bruno, would like to kill his father. At one point as he talks he seems to Guy 'to be growing indefinite at the edges, as if by some process of deliquescence'. He too, it appears, is some kind of borderline, a dark angel eager to draw out and feed on the darkness in others. Dimly, Guy recognises the signs: 'He seemed only a voice and a spirit now, the spirit of evil,' and yet for all his repugnance he can't quite shrug off his fascination. Finally Bruno comes out with his famous proposition, a variation on the Green Knight's: "'I kill your wife and you kill my father! We meet on the train, see, and nobody knows we know each other. Perfect alibis! Catch?"'

Only now, confronted a little too nakedly with his own fantasy, does Guy tear himself away from Bruno's sickly sweet force field, violently rejecting the proposition. But a connection has been opened, a powerful linkage underpinned by a half-conscious sexual attraction between them and by the disclosure (if only to himself) of Guy's murderous impulses.

The two part in Santa Fe with no agreement and no intention, on Guy's side, of ever seeing Bruno again. But before long Bruno, cheerfully infatuated with Guy and obsessed with cementing their alliance, decides to carry out his side of the proposal anyway. Tracking down Miriam, he follows her to an amusement park, where he approaches her in the darkness and strangles her. On the practical level this rids Guy of a threat to his future happiness. But on the more occult plane, the murder has the effect of merging Bruno and Miriam together, concentrating their respective capacities for evil into a single, composite figure whose ability to harm Guy is now immeasurably magnified.

Guy, hearing of the murder, hopes that it has nothing to do with Bruno but knows in his heart that it does. Should he tell the police? Of course he should. But how is he to explain Bruno's fiendish proposal without the risk of incriminating himself? An unblemished reputation, needless to say, is crucial to both his marriage and his chosen career. The police appear to believe the murder was an act of random violence, so why not let sleeping dogs lie? His sin at this point is purely one of omission. Nobody asked, so why should he tell? And what is there to tell anyway? Not only had he not entered into any kind of agreement with Bruno, but he had also explicitly denied to Bruno having ever had any desire to kill Miriam. So what if Bruno had divined that this was less than the truth? One is unanswerable for one's actions in this life, and possibly also for one's words, but not, surely, for the desires and fantasies that pass through one's mind unbidden, unarticulated and unacted on.

Well, apparently one is answerable for these too, at least to the Brunos and Nasreens of this world. Having killed Miriam, Bruno, who has a genius for rationalising matters to suit his own fancies, now considers he is owed a murder by Guy, but Guy understandably declines.

And so the stalking begins: Bruno phoning at odd hours, leaving messages with Guy's mother, his colleagues, his clients; Bruno appearing at Guy's office, outside his apartment, in the woods next to the house (the fortress) Guy is building for himself and Anne. Bruno sending emails, or rather letters, every two or three days: 'either a gush of brotherly love or a threat to haunt Guy all his life, ruin his career . . .'

One morning (and here the story melts into my own in a scene I still find unbearable to think of) Guy gets a call from a man who is about to hire him for an important job:

' "Mr. Haines . . . we've received a most peculiar letter concerning you . . ." '

Listening to the letter – identical to Nasreen's in spirit if not its literal content (allegations that Guy had a role in Miriam's death) – Guy grasps, for the first time, the extent of the malignancy that has attached itself to him:

'It would only be a matter of time until Bruno informed the next client, and then the next . . .'

Bruno, on the face of it, is harassing Guy for a very specific reason: to get him to kill his father. Whereas Nasreen – what did Nasreen want from me? Was there something I could have done or said that would have stopped her attacks once they began? Suppose I had handed over the keys to our apartment, or given her the money she occasionally demanded, or suppose I'd publicly confessed to being part of a Jewish conspiracy to steal her work and sell it to those other Iranian writers – would she have left me alone? I don't think so; certainly not if Highsmith is a reliable guide. Goaded beyond endurance (and the book enters a realm of darkness here that the film evades), Guy finally surrenders to Bruno's demands and kills Bruno's father. All goes well, in the sense that he gets away with it, and for a while Bruno leaves him alone. But even though any further contact with Guy at this point would be insanely dangerous for both of them, Bruno can't help himself. Because what he really wants – what he, like all such afflicted souls, fundamentally believes he is owed from Guy – is love; not the Lawrentian love that thrives on the separateness of the beloved, but the love that consumes him, dissolving him into the lover totally and for all eternity. Guy and Anne's wedding day comes around, and as Guy walks up the aisle, there is Bruno, smiling. 'Bruno was here with them, not an event, not a moment, but a condition, something that had always been and always would be.'

That was how I had come to see Nasreen by this time: not an event, not a moment, but a condition.

The surprise of the book is its unexpected compassion. Even at his most tormented, Guy continues to acknowledge something human and touching at the core of his tormentor: a vulnerability, even a kind of warped honesty, that sets him apart from other people and deserves its own kind of recognition, even its own kind of love. I can't say I've felt any of those things for Nasreen since she became my enemy, but at odd moments I have sensed that this is a failing on my part, maybe the precise failing that laid me open to her siege in the first place, and that perhaps if I could summon such feelings, the great sense of injustice lodged inside her, whatever its source, would stand a chance of being salved. But then I think of how she reacted to Paula's attempt at compassionate engagement, and I feel, once again, confronted by something unassuageable and beyond all understanding: a malice that has no real cause or motive but simply is.

Early in the summer I arrived home one afternoon to find a message from Detective Bauer. I phoned him at the precinct.

'I got a call from the lady,' he said.

I tried to sound uncomplicatedly pleased: 'That's great!'

'I figured she'd get around to it, sooner or later.'

'You were right.'

The detective cleared his throat. 'She was extremely angry. She used a lot of bad language. I don't like that.'

I asked what she was angry about.

'She didn't appreciate getting messages from her relatives to call the cops. That was a part of it.'

'What else?'

'Well, she certainly seems to believe you stole her work.'

I didn't think I needed to remind the detective how crazy Nasreen's conspiracy theories were.

'I guess she convinced herself,' I said.

There was a pause.

'Is it true you used to teach at Princeton?'

'Yes.'

'But not any longer?'

'Well, not at the moment.'

'She says you were fired for doing the same thing there. Taking students' work and selling it to other writers. She told me this is a well-known fact.'

I had predicted a counter-attack, but as always the sheer brazen outrageousness of Nasreen's malice caught me off my guard. A reeling sensation took hold of me. I heard myself explaining to the detective that I had taught on a casual basis at Princeton for twenty years, usually just for a term or two at a time, often with several years between appointments. I assured him my relations with the faculty

152

there were good, that I certainly hadn't stolen or been accused of stealing students' work, that there was no particular reason why I wasn't teaching there at the moment, and that I would be more than happy for him to call the writing department to verify all this. But even as I spoke I felt, again, the strange thinness and feebleness of my words in the face of Nasreen's. It wasn't that the detective was telling me he believed her, necessarily, but he had apparently felt unable to dismiss out of hand the possibility that a black market in students' stories was a part of the fabric of the creative-writing industry, with desperate authors buying up workshop submissions from unscrupulous instructors, and that I was a known dealer. He listened in silence while I spoke, and his response, when I had finished, was dismayingly non-committal. I offered several times to give him the number of the Princeton writing department, but he ignored me: not, I felt, because he took my word, but because he had decided not to get any more deeply involved in this dubious affair.

The one thing that seemed to count unequivocally against Nasreen was her 'bad language', which upset the detective as much as her casual references to drug-taking had earlier. It amazed me that an American cop, even one as buttoned-up as Detective Bauer, could be upset by 'bad language'. But he mentioned it disapprovingly several times, and as far as I could tell this unusual sense of decorum was the main reason why he had decided to continue regarding me as the victim, even if he was no longer sure I was guiltless.

'Anyway,' he said, 'I warned her if she contacted you or any of your colleagues ever again, we'd have her arrested for aggravated harassment.'

I thanked him. 'Do you think she'll stop now?'

'Well, I asked if she wanted to spend the rest of the summer locked up in a New York jail, and she said she definitely didn't want to. So I'm guessing she'll stop.'

'And if she doesn't?'

'I can talk to the DA, but like I said, I don't think he's going to extradite her from California on a misdemeanour.'

'So if she ignores your warning, there's really nothing else anyone can do?'

I was pushing him, but I had a feeling it wasn't going to be easy to get hold of the detective again after this conversation.

'We'll have to see. Maybe we can have a squad car drop by where she lives and talk to her. That's a possibility.'

'I should call you, then, if she sends any more emails?'

'Like I say, I think she'll stop, but if she does continue, then sure, go ahead and fax me the emails, and we'll see what else we can do. All right, Mr Lasdun?'

I hung up, telling myself that on balance this was good news. But I was depressed, all the same. Among other things, Nasreen had made it clear (so it seemed to me) that she now had my connection to Princeton in her sights. Did that mean she had sent them an email denouncing me as a thief and sexual predator like the one she'd sent Frank? I realised, with a kind of weary dread, that I was going to have to call the head of the writing department there to find out. I did: she hadn't sent anything, but if anything this made the conversation with my old colleague even weirder and more embarrassing than it would have been if she had. A lifetime of such conversations was what seemed to lie ahead of me if Detective Bauer's warning should fail.

There was silence for a few days. I allowed myself to feel fractionally encouraged. Then a YouTube forwarding arrived: a PJ Harvey video with the heading: '**ever hear of email blocking? This is my farewell email. Bye!**' Aware of how precarious my own mental condition was, I tried to take this as a good sign; proof that Detective Bauer had made an impression on Nasreen and that, in her incomparably annoying way, she was disengaging. Twenty minutes later another PJ Harvey video arrived. There was no message but the title of the song, 'Bitter Little Bird', seemed significant. Again, I told myself it was encouraging: a little rueful acknowledgement that she had come to the end of the road. Then a song called 'Rid of Me', also by PJ Harvey, arrived, along with the heading: '**last one . . . promise. tee hee.**' The taunting note was unmistakable, and the next couple of forwardings confirmed beyond doubt that any sense of defeat she may have initially felt after Detective Bauer's call was giving way to mocking defiance. '**you are under arrest for sending pj harvey videos!**' read the first; the second: '**You'll extradite me to ny for pj harvcy videos. that's sooooo nazi like.**' And by the end of the day she was back in full cackling cry. The video was Jay-Z's 'Breathe Easy', the message: '**ha ha ha ha.**'

I had been afraid of what would happen to me, psychologically, if the time came when I could no longer convince myself I was going to be able to make the emails stop. Now that time appeared to have come. Not that Detective Bauer's warning had had no effect at all: the emails did slow down after that initial deluge, and there were days, sometimes whole weeks, when I didn't hear from Nasreen. And for a long period the emails themselves became more oblique, less often overtly threatening. But by this time it was neither the content nor the frequency of the emails that mattered to me, so much as the mere fact of their continued existence. In my hypersensitised state, all it took was the sight of Nasreen's name or one of her many pseudonyms in my inbox to send me into a state of anxiety that could last all day. I was being given notice, it seemed to me, that there was nothing in my power that could bring an end to this torment. It was one thing to indulge in a kind of medicinal imagining of the worst, saturating myself in Patricia Highsmith while knowing that Detective Bauer was on the case, but now there was no longer any comforting frame of provisionality around the facts, and they were stark. The illness I had contracted was incurable. My adversary was stronger than I was. In abstract that sounds like a useful lesson for a man to learn, midway through life's journey, but it is hard nevertheless, and one learns it only with great bitterness and pain.

I put off calling Detective Bauer for some time, mainly because I didn't want to extinguish the last, faint, doubtless illusory flicker of hope that the thought of him still held out. I also disliked playing the role of the timid citizen who entrusts every aspect of his well-being to the forces of law and order, rather than defending them himself. But the logic of the situation seemed to have been steadily embedding the mask of that helpless figure into my own features ever since the drama began.

When I finally called the detective he was away, but he left a message a few days later, asking me to fax him the new emails. I did. Weeks passed with no word from him. I called again and was put through to his voicemail. The desk sergeants who answered the phone all knew my voice by now, and I felt I had become a laughing stock at the station: the poor persecuted professor. I hung up without leaving another message.

Winter arrived. In March 2009 I read an article in the *New York Times* about an identity theft case being prosecuted by the Manhattan DA, Robert Morgenthau, that bore some resemblance to my own. The setting was academe: an embattled biblical scholar whose overzealous son had assumed the identity of one of his father's critics and begun posting online messages in that person's name, 'admitting' to plagiarism from the father's work. '"This exemplifies a growing trend in the area of identity theft,"' the article quoted an assistant DA as saying. The son had been charged with identity theft, criminal impersonation and aggravated harassment, and faced up to four years in prison if convicted. I cut out the article and faxed it off to Detective Bauer, with a long letter explaining its relevance. He didn't respond. I concluded, perhaps unfairly, that he had decided he had done all he could do in this strange affair.

I couldn't altogether say that I blamed him.

Part IV

— — — — — — —

Mosaic

I am uneasy when confronted with my own work . . .
—Freud, *Moses and Monotheism*

I n the year 1700 a group of Polish Jews emigrated to Jerusalem. The journey was hard and by the time they arrived they were in ill health and penniless. Borrowing money from the Arab community, they built a synagogue in the Jewish Quarter, not far from the Wailing Wall. But their leader died, and before long they defaulted on their debt and the creditors burned down the building. Ever since then, the site it stood on has been known as the 'Hurva', which is the Hebrew word for 'ruin'.

For more than a century the ruin lay undisturbed, and then in 1864 a second synagogue was built on the same site, this time by Lithuanians, followers of the influential rabbi known as the Vilna Gaon: the 'Genius of Vilnius'. Their version of the building, designed for them by the Turkish sultan's own architect and modelled on the domed and arched mosques of Constantinople, dominated the skyline of the Jewish Quarter for almost a century and came to be regarded as the official synagogue of Old Jerusalem. Theodor Herzl spoke there. The first British high commissioner, Sir Herbert Samuel, paid a ceremonial visit in 1920. But in 1948, during the War of Independence, it too was destroyed, blown up by the Jordanian army as they took the Old City.

The Vilna Gaon, a revered figure in Orthodox Judaism, left behind a prophecy stating that three versions of the Hurva synagogue would be built, and that completion of the third would bring about the rebuilding of the Great Temple in Jerusalem. The rebuilding of the Temple is a dream cherished by all sorts of religious cults and associated, variously, with the arrival of the Jewish Messiah, the Second Coming of Christ, the Rapture and the End of Days.

In 1967, during the Six Day War, the Israelis captured the Old City and set about reconstructing the Jewish Quarter, which had been largely flattened. The project was overseen by the mayor of Jerusalem, Teddy Kollek, a cultured, liberal figure, legendary for his expansive spirit and tireless energy. In time Kollek turned his attention to the rubble of the Hurva synagogue and proposed yet another incarnation: the fateful third.

His ambitions for this version were grandly international. It would be both a civic and an architectural statement; a showcase for his vision of a reunited, enlightened, globally minded new Jerusalem. The first architect he appointed was the American pioneer of modernism Louis Kahn, who worked on it until his death in 1974. His plans were admired but not, in the end, adopted, and the project went dormant. But in 1978 Kollek took it up again, appointing a new architect, to whom he spelled out his rather exalted vision of the building:

'I fully believe that we will witness the creation of a religious and spiritual focus for world Jewry.'

The new architect was my father. For several years he shuttled back and forth between London and Jerusalem, working almost exclusively on the project. He wasn't especially religious (and though he always thought of himself as a Jew, and publicly identified as one, his Jewishness was complicated by the fact that he was also a baptised Christian). But he had a sort of agnostic regard for the possibility of higher mysteries, especially as embodied in the great churches and temples of antiquity. Ceremonial spaces fascinated him; he was responsive to the 'numinous' (a favourite word of his) in both nature

160

and architecture, and had always wanted to design a religious build-ing. Like Kahn, he devoted considerable time and energy to resolving the question of what a Jewish cathedral (for it was to be essentially that) could possibly look like at this late date in the ancient city. Like Kahn, he produced an uncompromisingly modernist design. And, like Kahn's, it came to nothing.

Some time before the project fizzled out, he took me aside to show me a letter he had been sent at his office. He had published his design in the *Architectural Review*, and the letter consisted of a photo-copy of the article with violent anti-Semitic abuse scrawled all over the pages. I had never seen anything like it in my life (I was in my early twenties). It was like a splinter from a block of some concen-trated substance that I had only ever known by rumour or, at most, in the much diluted form it took in polite English society, where oc-casionally someone would use the word 'Jewish' to mean tight with money. We stared at it together, and then my father put it away, ask-ing me not to mention it to my mother.

I remembered this letter when Nasreen's attacks began, and I thought of it many times as they continued. Overt anti-Semitism is rare today, and it seemed to me noteworthy that my father and I, neither of us exactly representative Jews, had both been at the re-ceiving end of it.

And yet what did it mean, this coincidence? A part of me sensed that, objectively speaking, it didn't mean anything at all. Certainly I didn't want to interpret it as evidence that anti-Semitism exists ev-erywhere, seething under veneers of strained civility. That way of thinking, always tempting to members of minority groups, is a dan-gerously easy way of blaming all one's woes on other people, and strikes me as something one should resist, even when it seems justified.

But meanwhile another part of me remained fixated on this curi-ous recurrence, and continued probing it as if it were some enigmatic legacy that might turn out to be valuable if I could only figure out what it was. When you are under acute stress, and when the source of your tribulation seems to lie beyond the reach of rational understanding, you start to attach great importance to any circumstance that resonates with your own. These things become your signs: the clues that, if you follow them correctly, will enable you (so you believe) to penetrate the mystery that stands before you.

In March 2010, an unexpected chain of events occurred that seemed, in conjunction with my father's letter, to comprise precisely such a sign, linking my father's very public field of action with my own largely private one, in ways that I found irresistibly fascinating.

It began with an announcement by the Israeli government of plans to build an extensive new settlement in East Jerusalem. Vice President Joseph Biden happened to be in Israel for peace talks at the time, and the announcement set off a major diplomatic row. I wasn't following the story closely, but after a few days a subplot emerged that involved, of all things, the Hurva synagogue, and I found myself suddenly paying attention.

Teddy Kollek had died in 2007, having retired from politics years earlier, and I'd assumed the Hurva project had long been forgotten. But apparently it hadn't. After all these years, the synagogue had finally been rebuilt: not as a modern building but as an exact copy, a 'stone for stone' replica (so the papers were reporting) of its Ottoman predecessor. It was about to be officially reopened, and the news, which had immediately become entangled with the settlement announcement, was provoking furious reactions from Palestinians. Hamas had called for a 'day of rage' to protest the rededication. Fatah accused the Israelis of 'playing with fire'. The spokesmen for both organisations referred explicitly to the Vilna Gaon's prophecy. In light of it, they claimed, the rebuilding of the synagogue amounted to a statement of intent to rebuild the ancient Temple, and was therefore to be regarded as a deliberate act of aggression towards the two sacred Muslim shrines that currently occupy the Temple Mount, or Haram Ash-Sharif (as Muslims call it): namely the Dome of the Rock and the Al-Aqsa Mosque. Arab Knesset members warned of a third intifada. Three thousand security personnel were put on alert for the opening ceremony.

The more I read, the more interested I became. In the thick gloom that had settled on me in the wake of Nasreen's attacks, it appealed to me, perversely, to discover a family connection to so promisingly apocalyptic an affair.

By this time I had already begun to consider writing something about Nasreen. My motive, initially, was purely defensive, and there was one particular incident that triggered it. I had been invited to apply for a teaching job at another college near where I live, and was updating my résumé when an email arrived from Nasreen. In it was a link to a website where she had posted a long article about the traumas she'd endured at the hands of her 'puffed-up former writing professor', who had 'won expensive prizes for "writing" stories based on my deteriorating state'; et cetera, et cetera.

Arriving at just this moment, the message had seemed to confirm my worst forebodings: that if I was offered this or any other job, it would only be a matter of time before Nasreen contacted the college and I would have to relive the mortifying scenes I'd been through with my other employers.

I was about to give up on the application when it occurred to me that if I had a website of my own, I could post the story of Nasreen, complete with sample emails, and refer people to it when the need arose. It wouldn't protect me against the taint that clings to one merely by being accused of certain crimes, but at least it would spare me some of the unpleasantness of having to explain the situation over and over.

I did create a website, jameslasdun.com (it seemed a miracle that Nasreen hadn't already appropriated the domain name), but somehow I couldn't get the tone right for the story. Just as I'd found when I'd talked to the FBI, the harder I tried to be neutral and objective, the crazier I sounded. Even the material I did post, some basic author information, comes off as a little obsessional, I realise now. 'This is the official website of the writer James Lasdun,' it begins, 'and the only reliably accurate source of information about his work . . .' I have left it up: a memorial to my brush with paranoia.

But in the process of trying to create this posting, I began to sense that if I cared to examine certain aspects of the story in greater depth than I was aiming for in that purely forensic account, then it had the potential to release the kind of large energies that could fuel a book – a book that would interest me, both as writer and as reader: wide-ranging, unpredictable, but unified by a single, elemental conflict.

It would be a risky enterprise: that was clear from the start. On top of the usual problems associated with writing any book, there would be some less routine matters to address. The necessity of using private emails in a story about accusations of plagiarism and violations of privacy was an irony I was going to have to come to terms with. I would also, needless to say, have to have the full consent of my wife and family before proceeding. I wouldn't have survived this ordeal without K——'s steadfast support, and I certainly wasn't going to jeopardise this by publishing a book against her wishes (she agreed to it without hesitation). Then too, there would be legal considerations that would have to be very thoroughly looked into (and resolved) with the cooperation of any potential publisher. Even if I settled all these matters for myself, there were bound to be readers – honest ones as well as the professionally offended – who would object to the very notion of such a book, and this was something I knew I would have to accept in advance. And finally, as one

of the lawyers I consulted pointed out, there would be the question
of how Nasreen herself might retaliate. Might I be making things
worse for myself? 'She'll do everything she can to discredit you,'
the lawyer warned. But hadn't she already? Certainly it was hard to
imagine anything more damaging than the allegations she had already made. And since those allegations – of plagiarism, of 'daytrading' her work with my Jewish cabal, of 'setting up' her rape at
the magazine where she worked before I taught her at Morgan College, and all the rest of it – were pure fabrication, wouldn't the daylight of publication be the best way of turning them to dust?

I hadn't kept copies of all my emails to her during the early phase
of our correspondence, but she had (or so she claimed), and these
would certainly prove that I'd liked her and had been warmly sup-
portive of her work. But there was nothing in them that embarrassed
me to remember (certainly nothing more embarrassing than the
ones I did keep and have already quoted). Still, I had to assume,
knowing her, that she would try to think of some way of using them
against me, and I realised I would have to resign myself to this too.

Despite all these obvious hurdles, the more I thought about the
project the more compelling it became. Nasreen's uncanny ability to
get under my skin – all the little neuroses and insecurities of mine
that she had so cleverly intuited and exploited – made her, potentially, an extremely illuminating subject as far as my interest in these
murky aspects of myself was concerned. There would be the arma-
ture of the case itself, but beyond it, if I could get it right, would be a
larger story woven from memories, journeys, portraits, observations
– all the stray psychic material that had been drawn into orbit
around the drama that had monopolised my consciousness for
more than three years now. I saw a place in it for my family, my
father, our Provence trip, my train ride across the country, my interest in questions of moral culpability, honour and reputation, desire
and repression; for various figures out of history, legend and fiction,

for an analysis of what it feels like to be a middle-aged white male writer of impeccable (by his own reckoning) liberal convictions, publicly accused of the tawdriest kinds of misconduct, and for an account of what happens when an unbelieving, not even entirely kosher Jew finds himself subjected to a firestorm of unrelenting anti-Semitism.

All of which, I am willing to concede, may have been merely the false excitement of desperation: the knowledge that I had to do *something* if I wasn't going to jump off a bridge, that writing was what I knew how to do best, and that at this point the only subject I was capable of writing about was Nasreen.

Even before the Hurva story appeared in the papers, I had begun to feel I should go to Jerusalem before writing this book. My idea was to situate myself at the geographic and spiritual heart of Judaism so that I could re-examine what I had experienced, from the viewpoint of maximum possible intimacy with the condition (so abstract to me) of being Jewish.

Specifically, I had an image of myself at the Western Wall (formerly the Wailing Wall), the stones of which were held by true believers to contain the Divine Presence, the *Shechina*; its earthly refuge pending the rebuilding of the Great Temple itself. I would stand at the Wall at sundown on Shabbat, wrapped in the force field of sacred observance distilled there down through the ages, and think about my long and strange ordeal.

But I am not in a position to 'situate myself' in some distant city just because I believe it might be useful for a book. Even if I had been, I would still have had to overcome my by-now leaden state of inertia, not to mention my private taboo against projects driven by acts of will rather than forces of necessity. So I mulled it over, vaguely wishing I could be teleported to Jerusalem but doing nothing about it.

Then out of the blue a magazine editor emailed to ask if I had any ideas for an article. This kind of invitation comes my way only rarely (in fact the last journalistic assignment I'd had was the one I'd taken the train to LA to write, several years earlier), so it was inevitable that this too should strike me as more than merely fortuitous: vindication, in fact, of my principle of passive acquiescence; the outer world knocking at my door just when I needed it, and for just the right reason. (This feverish, dubiously founded enthusiasm was increasingly my state of mind in those months.) I wrote back proposing an article on the Hurva synagogue. It would be a story of politics, history and architecture, I told the editor; part memoir, part essay, part travelogue. I would need to go to London first, to look at the Hurva papers in my father's archive, and then of course I would have to go to Jerusalem . . . It seemed politic to mention that I had other reasons, besides this article, for wanting to go there, and I told the editor about Nasreen (I was also concerned that she would send the magazine something unpleasant about me after the article came out, and I wanted to pre-empt that). He was interested; we even discussed bringing her into the piece. In the end I decided not to, but it helped to know that my motives were all, so to speak, out in the open. I have become pedantically scrupulous about such things.

A few weeks later I was on a plane.

In London I spent a day looking at my father's archive in the Victoria and Albert Museum. (A strange hilarity rises in me as I write those words: 'my father's archive in the Victoria and Albert Museum' – the way that faintly delirious note of grandeur seems to attach itself to every aspect of my father's life . . . In himself he was a stormy, passionate, embattled person, often laid low with depression. But around this volatile core radiated a paradoxical air of almost imperious serenity. There was the vulnerable human being, lying flat out in darkness on the living-room sofa, nursing his wounds after some attack in the press, but there was also this figure for whom a kind of imperturbable kingliness was somehow a given, the element in which his essential self existed. I lived in England until my late twenties, and it seemed wherever I went one of his buildings was always nearby. They were part of the geographic, almost the geological, foundation of my own existence. When I worked in Bloomsbury I would pass the School of Oriental and African Studies or another of his University of London buildings on my way to lunch. When I lived in Highgate my journey to my girlfriend in south London would take me past the Royal College of Physicians in Regent's Park, Hallfield School in Paddington, then the National Theatre and IBM headquarters on the South Bank. When I visited friends in Cambridge, Fitzwilliam College or Christ's would loom over us on and off all day as we wandered around. The vast scale and austere surfaces of these buildings, not to mention the fact that they were mostly 'controversial', which meant that my filial pride was always in danger of being affronted by someone saying something extremely rude about them, made their presence in my mind all the more charged and gigantic, while their frequently pyramidal form gave them, and by extension their maker, an inescapably Pharaonic aspect. Looking back, I realise how unusual it is for anyone, even a successful architect, to permeate the physical fabric of his world to quite this extent. But my father somehow conveyed, without any arrogance or posturing, that it was entirely in the natural course of things for him to have done this, and for a very long time this was how I saw it too. He and his buildings were natural phenomena to me, like mountains and plains. Even now, knowing how very remarkable and *un*natural it all was, how hard he had to fight for everything he accomplished, how much uncertainty and self-doubt he lived with, I can't quite shake off the traces of that other, regally entitled aura he projected. So it is impossible for me to speak casually of his 'archive in the Victoria and Albert Museum' without smiling

168

at my involuntary compliance in the illusion, as if it really is normal and unremarkable and altogether to be expected to have one's papers taken in by the V&A after one's death.)

The archivist had set out the Hurva material – five black box-files – in the architectural collection's study room. The files were full of notes, minutes, scribbles and correspondence covering everything from payment schedules to the comparative architectural traditions of Judaism and Christianity. There was plenty of dramatic material for my article: clashes and reconciliations by telex between my father and Teddy Kollek; minutes from meetings with Israeli diplomats in London and government officials in Jerusalem; press cuttings charting the progress of the job from the cornerstone-laying ceremony conducted with the president of Israel to its final fading away as it became clear that the prime minister, Menachem Begin, wanted a replica rather than a modern building (eighteen years after his death, the will of this deeply conservative leader appears to have prevailed).

And the letter was there, the hate letter my father had shown me in 1982. It was in a large white envelope. A swastika was drawn on the outside, so my father must have had a pretty good idea of what he was going to find inside. Gingerly, I took out the photocopied article it had been written on. Every single line of the article had been individually blacked out (I had forgotten this detail). 'AL QUDS, NOT THIS' was written at the top ('Al Quds' is the Arab name for Jerusalem). Next to it was a name, presumably the sender's, also in large, emphatic letters: 'JAWEED KARIM'. Scrawled over the pictures of my father's plans and models were phrases such as 'DANGER JEWS ABOUT' and weird punning insults: 'HOMOSEXUALS USE SINAGOG', and so on. There were drawings of swastikas equaling Stars of David, such as you see on protest banners today, and there was an outright threat: 'IF YOU DESIGN THIS YOU WILL DIE PREMATURE DEATH.' There was also the peculiar conflation of the roles of victim and oppressor that seems to distinguish anti-Semitism from other forms of racism, and that was such a pronounced feature of Nasreen's emails: 'HITLER WAS RIGHT TO GAS JEWS', on the one hand, and on the other: 'THIS IS JEW ECONOMY DIRTY PEOPLE ONLY KNOW HOW TO MASSACRE PEOPLE.'

From London I flew to Israel, arriving in Jerusalem at dusk. Ramadan was in its last week, and the city was quiet. My hotel, a former private villa, was in East Jerusalem, the Arab part of the city. It had been recommended as a place to meet interesting people: NGO workers, journalists, political operatives with connections on both sides of the conflict. The idea of subjecting my tribal allegiances to a slight geographic torsion was also a part of the appeal.

I was tempted to stay in for the evening, unwind in the candlelit garden bar, but I made myself go out. The concierge gave me directions to the Old City, a fifteen-minute walk. The streets were dark, almost empty. Two days earlier a settler's car had been ambushed, all four passengers shot dead, and although it had happened in the West Bank, several miles from Jerusalem, it was different thinking about it here on Nablus Road than it had been reading about it in my mother's kitchen in London. I walked quickly.

More people appeared as the Old City's medieval wall came into view. Lights flared on the steps leading down to the Damascus Gate, and there were vendors selling kebabs and candy to the crowds breaking their fast for the day. A man was inflating silver balloons from a rust-streaked helium tank in the centre. Another man handed out fluorescent soft drinks in plastic bags. I passed through the gate onto El-Wad Road, one of the narrow thoroughfares running through the old Arab Quarter. A few lamps burned in storefronts, but most of the little businesses had been shuttered for the night. Overhead, blue fairy lights strung between rooftops glinted against the black sky. Robed men, women in headscarves, groups of small children, moved along the narrow street. The air was warm, full of cooking smells and bursts of sound from radios: Arab pop and the distorted wail of prayers being chanted through megaphones. A glow appeared and around a corner a dozen men sat on rickety chairs outside a store with a single naked bulb, smoking narghiles. They stared at me as I passed, and I stared back, noting their tender, creaturely involvement with the pipes: the long, coiling, tail-like tubes held in one hand, the smoke bubbling through the murky stomachs of water.

I ate in a small restaurant and wandered on into a maze of alleys, unsure whether or not to be concerned about the darkness. As I turned onto what must have been the Souk Khan al-Zeit road, heading back towards the Damascus Gate, three Orthodox Jews, a father and two sons in black hats and coats, appeared just ahead of me; the father full-bearded and portly, the sons in knee breeches, sidelocks dangling against their pale cheeks. It surprised me to see them there, in the heart of the Arab Quarter. As I followed behind them it occurred to me that they were possibly from one of the national-religious factions I'd read about who had taken over buildings in East Jerusalem. They moved purposefully along the street, with what seemed a certain deliberately unwatching watchfulness. Out of the gate, they cut sharply up through the crowds on the steps. A loud bang came from the centre and for a second I thought it was a gunshot, but it was a helium balloon bursting, and the three moved on without flinching, disappearing across the street above.

In the morning, Misha, a friend of a friend, gave me a tour of the city. Misha had grown up partly in America and moved to Jerusalem a few years earlier. He was a writer and translator, also a doctoral student with a half-finished PhD on Isaac Bashevis Singer's novel The

Penitent. I like Singer but I hadn't read this book. It was the story of a womanising businessman in America, Misha told me, who gives up everything to join the ultra-Orthodox Haredim after a visit to Jerusalem. I promised to read it, though it sounded a bit austere for my tastes.

We walked through the Old City, taking a meandering route that led past crumbling Mamluk palaces, down the Via Dolorosa with its dense crowds of Christian pilgrims bowed under heavy crosses, and into the Jewish Quarter. The buildings there were modern but faced in the ancient-looking sand-gold Jerusalem stone that was apparently statutory for all new construction. It was easy on the eye but created a slightly unreal, stage-set atmosphere. The human element added to the effect, consisting mostly of Haredim whose eclectic period gear, worn on a motor scooter or while chatting on a cell phone, seemed to collapse several eras into one. In Hurva Square we stopped to look at the new synagogue. It too was faced in Jerusalem stone, but of a whiter shade than its neighbours, which made it look eerily new, while its form – the shallow dome supported on a squat cube of four wide arches, with towers at each corner – was clearly antique, further compounding the sense of temporal confusion. I made some quick first-impression notes for my article, and we moved on.

Passing through the Jaffa Gate, we crossed into the wide, unshaded streets of the New City. At some point Misha described himself as socially liberal 'but pretty conservative on security'. Despite, or perhaps because of this, he was careful to draw my attention to various injustices of municipal policy as we walked around. In Silwan, he explained how building safety regulations had been exploited to justify the seizure and demolition of Arab homes. In Mamilla he showed me the intended location of the imprudently named 'Museum of Tolerance', where construction had been halted because of international protests over the siting of the building on top of a

Muslim cemetery. We talked about these protests, and the hostility that had been growing towards Israel in general over the past couple of decades: the academic boycotts, the consumer boycotts, the comparisons to South Africa under apartheid, and so on.

I had been thinking about these subjects quite a bit since Nasreen had begun her attacks. Israel and the Palestinians had been constantly in the headlines. There was the invasion of Gaza at the end of 2008, but all year bad news had been spilling out of the region. I felt implicated in the conflict in a way I never quite had before, and compelled to take a position, though at the same time I found it impossible to anchor myself in any stable point of view. The question of where honest criticism of Israel ended and anti-Semitism began had started to interest me greatly, perhaps because I was trying to determine the line where Nasreen's attacks on me, personally, crossed from legitimate grievance (at least in her mind) to deliberate, malicious smear. The boycott movement seemed bound up in this question, somehow, but I had to admit I had extremely confused feelings about it.

I remembered the story of the left-wing academic at Ben-Gurion University who had allegedly been told by the editors of the British journal *Political Geography* that an article he had written (co-written with a Palestinian academic, actually) would be accepted only if he included a statement in it comparing Israel to apartheid South Africa. Whatever one thought of the comparison, the stipulation seemed very obviously stupid and wrong. But not everything was as easy to dismiss, at least not for me. A few years ago, for instance, a petition was circulated by a group of architectural luminaries, calling for a boycott against architects involved in the 'settlement industry'. Among the signatories were several British Jews and at least one former colleague of my father's. I don't think my father would have signed it himself if he had still been alive (he seldom signed anything), but he would have been troubled by it, and receptive to its arguments, and I think it might have made him wonder if it wasn't just as well that his involvement with the Hurva project had ended when it did.

Of course, the rebuilding of a synagogue in the Jewish Quarter of the Old City could hardly be considered part of the 'settlement industry', so from that point of view he would have been in the clear even if his design had been built. Or so it would have seemed at the time. But according to a book I'd read in preparation for my article, even this was now open to question. The book, Simone Ricca's *Reinventing Jerusalem*, makes the very contentious case that the rebuilding of the Jewish Quarter after the Israelis captured the Old City in '67 was not the historically sensitive reconstruction of an 'already existing' neighbourhood that it purported to be, but rather a calculated, triumphalist exercise in the manufacture of Jewish 'heritage'. Kollek, in Ricca's hands, turns from enlightened visionary into a more stained and devious figure, hoodwinking the world into accepting the illusion of a much more substantial historic Jewish presence in the Old City than had ever in fact been the case. Using demolition, expropriation, selective archaeology and architectural *trompe l'oeil*, he and his colleagues created, according to Ricca, not a reconstruction at all but a settlement, the ur-settlement in fact: the practical model and indeed the spiritual inspiration for most of the settlements that followed in its wake (the unbroken connection to the old Jewish Quarter being an indispensable element in the historic claim to the Land of Israel). The Hurva synagogue, along with the newly cleared esplanade beneath the Western Wall, was intended to form the centrepiece of this 'settlement'. I can't say exactly how my father would have reacted if the project had been presented to him in these terms rather than Kollek's more nobly appealing 'focus for world Jewry', but I imagine he would have had some serious misgivings.

174

Whatever the case, the implications of this building seemed more incendiary than ever after I finished the book, and once again the thought of my (albeit tenuous) connection to it offered a certain gloomy satisfaction. This had to do with Nasreen, who was a constant presence in my mind during this trip. It seemed to confer a more dignified solemnity on our conflict, turning me into a larger, grander adversary, somehow, than her 'daytrading' conspiracy theory implied. Better to be found complicit in the original sins of Israeli history than in some act of petty plagiarism.

At some point, as Misha and I discussed the world's apparent fascination with Israeli politics, I repeated a line from Saul Bellow's book *To Jerusalem and Back*, which I was also reading for my article (it contains a vivid portrait of Teddy Kollek at the time of my father's involvement with him). 'What Switzerland is to winter holidays,' Bellow writes, '. . . Israel and the Palestinians are to the West's need for justice – a sort of moral resort area.'

Misha liked that. He repeated it approvingly: 'moral resort area'. He told me there was actually a well-organised 'moral tourism' industry in Israel these days, with bus trips to weekly protest venues all around the country. He knew of an Italian art professor who brought his students to the Sheikh Jarrah neighbourhood in East Jerusalem on a regular basis, for a class on protest photography. Seeing me write all this down in my notebook, Misha clarified his position. 'I'm not opposed to the protests themselves,' he told me, 'just to certain oversimplifications they encourage.' He began to lay out the complexities of the situation as he saw it, speaking with a curious inward-directed frown, as if he were arguing with himself while addressing me, and I glimpsed something that became increasingly evident as I spoke to other Jewish Israelis, namely the uncomfortably narrow margin a person of any moral sensitivity must have to operate within here: bounded between conscience on one side and, on the other, a natural reluctance to commit oneself to a line of reasoning that, pursued too far, would begin to place one in opposition to one's own existence.

Before we parted Misha took me to his favourite used-book store. We rummaged around, and by chance I came upon an old paperback of *The Penitent* on a dusty shelf near the back. It looked as forbidding as I'd imagined: a faded illustration of a bearded man in gabardine and fringed garment on the cover, along with a not very enticing quote from the *Chicago Tribune* describing it as the story of 'one who has returned to the faith of his fathers'. But I felt compelled to buy it all the same.

I spent the next few days interviewing people for my article. The architect of the newly replicated Hurva gave me a tour of the building. I went to Tel Aviv to talk to scholars and critics. Back in Jerusalem, an architectural historian who knew the complicated story of the building invited me to his house in the suburb of Malcha.

Before I set off, I googled the address and stumbled briefly into a universe of websites denouncing the Zionist takeover of what had once been an Arab village, al-Maliha.

The term 'ethnic cleansing' was used. I navigated away, but the phrase wasn't so easy to shake off. It is another of those contaminating terms, like 'apartheid' or 'rape', that trigger a very specific shunning reflex when you hear them: an urgent impulse to dissociate yourself from the person or group they are applied to, even if you question the validity of the application.

The phrase pulsed in my mind as I set off, tinged in the bloodlight of the Yugoslav massacres for which it was coined. Again I was aware of something connected with Nasreen – some trace or emblem of her that had by now taken up permanent residence in my own consciousness – clutching onto the two words with a kind of avid, triumphant tenacity. They seemed to shed their taint on everything I saw as my taxi cruised into Malcha: the quiet residential streets curving around their hilltop, the rows of shiny parked cars, the pedestrian-only enclave where the historian lived, with its stepped, bougainvillea-lined walkways, at the safe heart of which a lone boy my son's age was shooting hoops in the waning daylight.

The historian's house was compact and modern, with framed abstracts mounted alongside folk-art weavings and carvings. The historian himself gave an impression of wanting to seem more detached from the fray of Jerusalem politics than he really felt, and the result was an uneasy geniality punctuated by bursts of sardonic gloom.

He knew Teddy Kollek well – well enough to have had a public falling-out with him. 'He called me a clinical psychopath,' he remembered, smiling drily. He told me that he'd disliked Louis Kahn's design, and then added bluntly, 'I didn't like your father's design either.' Both, in his view, were too provocative – to aesthetically conservative Jews as well as politically wary Palestinians – to have stood any real chance of being built. There was also a short-lived third plan, he remembered, designed by an architect close to the ultra-Orthodox and backed by Ariel Sharon. 'Terrible,' he snarled, showing me a picture of a model that looked like a space helmet dipped in bronze. 'Dome of the Rock, Yiddish style . . .'

We got onto the subject of the Vilna Gaon's prophecy and Palestinian anger at the rebuilding of the synagogue. Was it possible, I asked, that the project really did amount to some kind of proxy action for rebuilding the Great Temple?

The question drew down another grimace across the historian's lined features. He nodded. 'For some people, yes.'

There was a thriving 'Third Temple' subculture in Jerusalem, he explained. Somewhere in the Old City was a basement full of proposed models for the building, each more lavish than the next. Funds could be raised to build any one of them in six months, he assured me gloomily, if any government was foolish enough to allow new construction on the Temple Mount.

This subculture was on the far fringe of the ultra-Orthodox movement, he was careful to add, but on the other hand there was probably no spot on earth where religious fantasy had more combustible potential than the small area in Old Jerusalem encompassing the mosques and the Western Wall. Ariel Sharon's visit to the Temple Mount in September 2000, a deliberately provocative assertion of Jewish prerogatives on what is now sacred Muslim ground, had set off the second intifada. An attempt to build on it could very easily ignite a third world war.

Breakfast in the leafy courtyard of my hotel. The guests at the other tables appear to be mostly Scandinavian or African. I stayed up late reading the Singer novel, which was unexpectedly gripping, and a residue of its narrator seems to be lingering over me, making me feel oddly conspicuous, as if his dark hat and ritual garment were glimmering spectrally over my Banana Republic T-shirt and khakis.

It surprises me to find myself hospitable to this character, Joseph Shapiro. I've had no serious religious feelings since I was a teenager, and have no interest in developing any. But before Shapiro becomes that pious figure on the book cover he is a regular flawed and fallen human being, which is of course what makes him appealing. Furthermore, in the process of transformation he undergoes his own version of precisely the trials I have felt ghosting my own ever since these events began. He too, it turns out, is a Gawain, a Lawrence, a Guy Haines.

The turning point in his story comes one night after he discovers he is being cheated on by both his wife and his mistress. All his vague disgust for the life of cheap titillation that he has been living in America boils up inside him, precipitating a crisis. Barely aware of what he is doing, he goes to the airport and buys a ticket to Israel, carrying nothing more than an overnight bag and a couple of religious books.

On the plane a young woman, Priscilla, sits down next to him, carrying a volume of Sartre. 'She smelled of eau de Cologne, chocolate, and other scents enticing to a male. I was reading about abstinence and sacred matters . . .'

She glances at his book and asks if the letters are Hebrew. They are, he replies. She had been sent to Hebrew lessons as a child, she tells him, but now the language 'is a completely strange element to me'. His reply is innocent enough on the surface: 'No matter how strange an element may be, it can become familiar,' but even as he speaks he acknowledges that his words 'carried a sly reference, as if to say "Now I'm a stranger, but tomorrow I may sleep with you."' The girl orders a whiskey. He joins her, assuring himself he is doing so purely out of politeness, but the dance has begun, the 'dere dalyaunce', and he is well aware of the real reason. She mentions a fiancé but at the same time lets Shapiro know that she doesn't believe couples are under any obligation to be faithful to each other. Shapiro, feeling the old sweet responsiveness rising inside him at this flagrant invitation, struggles to resist it. The adjacent seats have become his version of the room, the roomette, that private but violable space in which one's most intimate conflicts act themselves out: 'I sat there baffled by the dramatic turn of events my life had taken and by my own lack of character. I had abandoned everything to flee from the lie, but the lie now sat next to me, promising me who knows what joys . . .' It is cold on the plane, and at Priscilla's suggestion Shapiro spreads a blanket across his lap. Soon he feels her hand moving under the blanket. Their fingers touch, entwine, and at once they are entangled in a session of furtive petting and groping. But there are limits to what you can do on a plane, and after a while they pull apart, strangers again, Shapiro filled with rankling physical dissatisfaction while at the same time overcome with shame: 'We were left sitting there like two whipped dogs . . .'

Just then a man in full Orthodox garb walks down the aisle beside them. Priscilla, modern and assimilated, grimaces. 'Her eyes reflected embarrassment and scorn.' But to Shapiro the figure is a sign, a revelation that crystallises his hitherto rather vague spiritual yearnings into their final, inflexible form: 'I realised at that moment that without earlocks and a ritual garment one cannot be a real Jew. A soldier who serves an emperor has to have a uniform, and this also applies to a soldier who serves the Almighty. Had I worn such an outfit that night I wouldn't have been exposed to those temptations . . .'

It is proving difficult to find Palestinians willing to talk about the Hurva synagogue. I leave messages but nobody calls back. When I do finally make contact with someone, a professor of urban studies at Al-Quds University, his response is a volley of polite excuses: 'You see I am very busy now because Ramadan is coming to an end and I have many things to do but I wish you the best of luck with your article, goodbye.'

I mention the difficulty to a cousin of mine at her house in the German Colony, where she has lived since the seventies. She nods, unsurprised. She volunteers for an organisation that helps Palestinians with legal problems, but even this limited contact between the two communities has become strained in recent years, and increasingly rare. Contact of a purely social or intellectual nature is virtually impossible. She tells me the following story.

She and her husband were friendly with a Palestinian housepainter from Bethlehem who often did work for them. His wife needed dialysis and had a pass to get into Jerusalem for regular treatment at the Hadassah hospital. After the second intifada broke out, the twenty-minute drive from Bethlehem turned into a half-day trip with all the detours and checkpoints. Then, mysteriously, it became further complicated by entirely new bureaucratic obstacles. One day a mutual friend called my cousin with grim tidings: the Israeli authorities had made it impossibly difficult for the man to get his wife to the hospital and she had died. Furthermore, the man's son had been killed, shot dead while visiting a settlement to collect payment for a carpentry job.

Some time passed, and then the mutual friend called my cousin again. The circumstances of the son's death were not, after all, as he had first reported. The boy had in fact been shot in a supermarket, where he had been about to detonate a suicide vest. The father had been unable to come to terms with this fact, hence the version of events he had originally told the mutual friend, but it was indeed the case, and it was also the reason why the Israelis had made it so difficult for the mother to get her dialysis.

If I were writing the story I would want to end it there: a bleak equipoise of mutual ill will. But it doesn't end there. The man remarried and started a new family. A year later the army came with bulldozers and demolished his house.

The scene is convivial at the garden bar; most of the customers are on first-name terms with the barman, Fadi, who laughs obligingly at their banter as he mixes their drinks.

Next to me is a woman with stringy grey hair and weathered features, talking in Italian-accented English to a couple of Arab men in jackets and open shirts.

Listening in, I gather that she is a journalist and they are civic officials of some kind. I try to edge into the conversation, sensing an opportunity to get some impromptu Palestinian reaction to the Hurva. But my polite gestures and smiles go unnoticed, and I can't quite bring myself to do anything more forceful. I read the newspapers instead, peering at them in the dim candlelight. The *Herald-Tribune* has a story about the taxi driver in New York, Ahmed Sharif, who had his throat slashed by a passenger for being Muslim. *Haaretz* has an article on a poll released by the Spanish government showing that 'one in three Spaniards is anti-Semitic, maintaining negative opinions about Jews'.

By uncertain processes of association, I find myself thinking of another of Saul Bellow's remarks from his Jerusalem book, to the effect that 'even-handedness' is not a useful or even commendable attitude to take in this city. Visitors who are always judiciously observing on the one hand this and on the other hand that infuriate him. Support for the Jewish state, he implies, is worth nothing if it doesn't come out of strong emotional conviction, because the corrosive logic of the situation will eat away at any attitude founded on mere 'even-handedness', devouring arguments until there is nothing left. Better to be outright hostile.

I recognise that equivocating tendency in myself. So much depends on where you begin the story you are trying to tell, which in turn, as far as I can see, depends on whom you happen to like most, or dislike least. The army bulldozed the Palestinian's home. But his son tried to blow up a supermarket. But it was a supermarket on land illegally occupied by settlers. But the land was part of ancient Judaea. But the Jews have been absent from Judaea for more than two thousand years. But the Holocaust . . .

I make my way under dark palms to my room, in an annexe away from the main building. The air is warm, scented with night blossoms. As I reach the annexe door, a woman appears from another direction. We enter together and stand in the empty vestibule, waiting for the tiny elevator. She looks about thirty-five, black hair cut short, smooth pink cheeks. She seems a little uncomfortable, finding herself in this deserted space with a strange man. I smile, trying

182

to signal my harmlessness, and make a comment about the nice evening. She appears to relax. 'Isn't it gorgeous?' she says.

In the slow, creaking elevator, which we are both taking to the same floor, we exchange further remarks to cover up what would otherwise be an awkward silence. By the time we arrive at our floor we are having something more like a real conversation. She seems interested in the article I'm writing, and in fact subscribes to the magazine that commissioned it. She herself is here with an NGO that does psychiatric work in a Palestinian refugee camp in Ramallah. She goes to the door of her room, and I move along the narrow landing to my own door, but she seems to want to continue talking, and for several minutes we linger across the landing from each other, talking in the thin brass glare of the night lights. She lives in Atlanta, she says, but she comes here every year to work in the refugee camps. She likes to bring visitors, to show them what conditions are like for the Palestinians. 'I mean, I give them things to do, people to talk to. They don't stand around just staring.' 'It sounds interesting,' I say. 'You should come, if you have some free time.' 'Well, I'd like to.'

The hotel is moving her into the main building tomorrow, and she gives me the number of what will be her new room. 'I'm Nadia,' she says, opening her door. She is wearing a blue dress with white polka dots. I tell her my name. We smile at each other and say goodnight.

In my room I feel the encounter reverberating inside me, a pleasant after-effect in which the impression of her pink cheeks and blue dress are present, jumbled together with a feeling that I ought not to pass up an opportunity to visit one of these camps.

I write down the room number she gave me, intending to call her in the morning.

At the same time I am aware of something delicately treacherous in the air. The phrase 'moral resort area' rises up at me from the

Bellow book next to my bed. Beside it Joseph Shapiro grimaces from the cover of the Singer novel. I remember the way he describes his conversation with Priscilla on the plane, his unabashedly archaic terms: 'I knew very well that this was the Evil Spirit talking through her . . .'

I turn out the light, telling myself not to be ridiculous. Being happily married doesn't mean you have to behave like some misogynistic ascetic, any more than being Jewish means you can't look at things that reflect badly on Israel.

I had intended to spend the afternoon at Yad Vashem, the Holocaust museum, but I couldn't face it, and am in the Garden of Gethsemane instead, thinking about Judas Iscariot.

The garden is a small, enclosed olive grove with gravel paths leading among twenty or so olive trees. Some of these are said to be over two thousand years old. They are tremendously wide, like very large and ancient women, their twisting bodies at once bulbous and cavernous. Their silver-and-green leaves – all eyes, as the Greeks observed – wink in the breeze, and it is impossible not to think of the scene they witnessed when they were young. This is where Judas of the Thirty Pieces of Silver becomes Judas of the Kiss, the gesture transforming him from petty money-grubber into the great antagonist of the Passion, the necessary betrayer.

In Provence K—— and I and the kids did a walk that led along the Levens valley to the fifteenth-century Chapel of Notre Dame des Fontaines, a small white building in the middle of nowhere that happens to contain one of the great masterpieces of early Renaissance art, Giovanni Canavesio's fresco cycle of the Life of Christ.

Judas first appears in the panel depicting the Last Supper, where he sits in profile opposite Jesus, in blue-and-brown robes. Alone of all the company he has no halo, but his unruly reddish hair has something windswept and romantic about it, and his bearded profile, in contrast to the bland baby faces of the other disciples, is full of dashing individuality, with a hint of amusement about the lips and an appealingly manic exuberance in his eye. Apparently Jesus hasn't yet informed this fiery disciple of the ignominious role he has been chosen to play in the coming drama. He is gesturing eloquently, one arm raised high, clearly speaking about some matter of passionate concern to him. Jesus and the rest look at one another with uneasy sidelong glances.

One interpretation of 'Iscariot' identifies Judas as a member of the Sicarii, a group of Jewish assassins intent on driving the Romans out of Judaea, and there is a tradition of Judas as an insurrectionist who had hoped to win Jesus over to the cause of armed revolt against the occupying power. Certainly Canavesio would have known that Judas went in for political grandstanding. There is the incident in John where Judas scolds Jesus for allowing Mary of Bethany to annoint him with a whole pint of expensive perfume instead of making the woman sell it to help the poor. John is quick to assure the reader that this outburst isn't as noble as it might appear. According to him, Judas just wants to pilfer the money from the communal kitty, which he looks after: 'This he said, not that he cared for the poor; but because he was a thief, and had the bag, and bare what was put therein.' But the comment sounds suspiciously catty and after-the-fact revisionist (I can't help thinking of how Nasreen only started accusing me of theft after she had turned against me). At any rate, judging from Judas's upraised arm and the misgivings on the faces of his fellow diners, it would seem that the urging of some kind of extreme rebellious action is being imagined here by the painter.

But whatever cause Judas may be pleading, we can assume it finds no favour. In the next panel he stands with a chastened and troubled look, waiting in line as Jesus kneels down, washing his disciples' feet. Judas is lifting his leg to take off his sandal, a touchingly prosaic gesture that again contrasts with the attitudes of placid piety assumed by his fellow disciples. He seems torn: at once eager for the cleansing and a bit sullen about it. You sense that he has begun to feel, confusedly, the first inklings of his ordained role as betrayer stirring inside him, and is dimly attempting to ward it off, while at the same time beginning to find all this humility business (Jesus kneeling on the floor with his sleeves rolled up) irritating. At this point in the sequence he comes over as a case of the unstable artist-intellectual type: restless, querulous, contrarian, driven by conflicting urges, attaching himself to causes only to turn against them – an embodiment of nature's own principle of growth by division.

By the next panel his transformation has begun in earnest. A demon grips his purse ('Then entered Satan into Judas'), and in quick succession as you walk down the nave he is shown visiting the Temple in Jerusalem to negotiate his informer's fee with the priests, counting out an advance on the thirty pieces of silver, leading the Roman soldiers here into the Garden of Gethsemane, and then lightly kissing Jesus's half-averted face, one hand on Jesus's shoulder, the other stretched out backwards to receive the balance on his fee. His own face by now has begun to change, its hitherto fierce nobility turning into something altogether more rattish or wolfish.

He disappears for a while before turning up again on the other side of the nave. The panel, *The Remorse of Judas*, refers to the passage in Matthew where Judas, discovering that Jesus has been sentenced to death, repents and tries to return the thirty pieces of silver. The priests refuse it, and he flings the money onto the Temple floor, storming off: a grimacing, twisting study in impotent anguish and disbelief, as if, like Shylock, he has just had revealed to him the colossal cunning and malice of the trap his own avarice has led him into. It is a staggeringly un-Christian moment in the Gospel story – the repentant sinner whose sincere wish to make amends is flatly refused – and Canavesio highlights the cruelty with a little diabolic touch of his own, placing Jesus himself at the edge of the scene, apparently taking a moment out from his flagellation to make sure his enemy is given no encouragement to avoid the despair that will shortly consign his soul to hell for all eternity.

And next to this panel, juxtaposed with the impassive abruptness of the Gospel narrative itself ('And he cast down the pieces of silver in the temple, and departed, and went and hanged himself'), is the panel of Judas self-slaughtered: hanging by a rope from an olive tree, his abdomen split open with its contents hanging out.

The image actually combines two different accounts from the Bible: the guilt-stricken suicide from Matthew 27, and the unrepentant sinner of Acts 1 who buys real estate with his ill-gotten gains and dies entirely by accident, in a nasty fall (the land itself rising up against its usurper, so to speak): 'he burst asunder in the midst, and all his bowels gushed out.'

It is a terrifying picture, not so much for the dangling organs and guts as for the face, a greenish-hued rictus in which the agony of the victim and the rapacity of the evil-doer merge into an image of pure, free-floating horror, and I remember it vividly (it has come to form a private image of a certain familiar soul state, call it the state of ruin, as in 'I will ruin him'; swinging from a gibbet with one's insides spilling out for the world to see): the eyes all rolling whiteness with red-rimmed lower lids, the stiff tongue poking out between crooked fangs, hair and beard matted in greasy rats' tails, the grey-green ghetto pallor of the skin, the nose long and hooked; the whole physiognomy at last unambiguously and aggressively Semitic, or anti-Semitic (in certain contexts there is no distinction), as if in this climactic gesture of eternal self-exile from the community of man and the grace of God (he is dangling in a strange void, separated even from the tree he hangs from by a high wall guarding the verdant landscape behind him), he has finally become above all else Judas the Judaean, the archetype of the Jew in the medieval imagination, his name an incitement, a fatal convergence of interests.

I call Nadia. Three days have passed since we talked on the landing, but I haven't called her until now. I've picked up the phone a couple of times, and then thought better of it. But this morning I decided I had allowed the matter to become unnecessarily complicated, and that this was yet another symptom of Nasreen's effect on me.

I recognise the nice Southern voice when she says hello.

'Hey, Nadia, this is James. We met the other night. You offered to show me the refugee camp in Ramallah.'

'You have the wrong number.'

'This isn't Nadia?'

'No.'

I apologise and hang up, very unsure about what has just occurred. I didn't misdial the three-digit room number, and from what she told me earlier, she wasn't leaving Jerusalem any time soon. I suppose she must have given me the wrong number and I was mistaken in thinking I recognised her voice.

But I am fairly certain it was Nadia, and this makes me wonder if there was some disparity between what I experienced during our original encounter and what actually happened, some delayed effect of my words or manner that has caused her to have second thoughts about her invitation. This in turn awakens an ancient insecurity of mine: is there something about myself that I simply don't see?

Succumbing to a sort of piqued, lethargic mood, I lie on my bed looking at YouTube videos of refugee camps instead. Rubble and graffiti; a small child staring at a patrolling tank; an old woman saying that she would like to die. Clips from the weekly settlement protests appear in the portal and I drift on into these. Maale Adumim, Nabi Salih, Beit Jala, Silwan. They rouse violent, contradictory emotions. The spectacle of settlers clutching sacred texts as they assert their God-given right to land they have ousted Palestinians from is viscerally shocking. Even as you register the shock, though, you find yourself cringing at the uncanny way in which the rituals of modern protest recall the ancient gestures and geometries of Jew baiting: camera-wielding protesters getting in the faces of the religiously garbed, increasingly agitated settlers, pushing and goading them until they come out with the terrible thing – the racist comment, the fanatical religious self-justification – that will stand as their portrait, their panel, for as long as the living fresco-cycle of YouTube survives. Some of the videos are obvious anti-Israel propaganda. A few carry bluntly anti-Semitic titles. But even after you have made all possible allowances in that direction, even after you have noted the preening self-regard of some of the backpacking 'internationals' protesting alongside the Palestinian villagers and anti-settler Israelis, the sense that something calamitous is preparing itself in these dusty hilltops is overwhelming. You watch in dismay as a group of young male settlers in yarmulkes beat and kick a family of Palestinians who have come, with a judge's warrant, to harvest their olives. The army arrives and you think, Well, at least there is this. But then you watch the soldiers arrest not the young settlers, but the Palestinians. Dark forebodings rise up inside you. You begin to wonder if these settlers with their rifles and prayer shawls ('Guns 'n' Moses' is a popular T-shirt logo in Jerusalem) might not be enabling ancient impulses that once manifested themselves as straightforward bigotry, to regroup under the banner of justice.

And it comes to me that behind the figure of Judas stands that of Jacob, my implacably grasping namesake (the name means 'he who supplants'), tricking his brother out of his birthright, wrestling with the angel: 'I will not let thee go except thou bless me . . .' and then duly blessed; the blessing being life, more life, and with nothing dreamy or languidly abstract about it: pots and pans, flocks of sheep, olive groves, gemstones, weapons, women, offspring numberless 'as the stars of heaven'; land. Strange profile for a religious patriarch, as if the very hunger were its own theology: I want this more than you want it and that makes it mine.

'A work grows as it will and sometimes confronts its author as an independent, even an alien creation . . .'

The words are from Freud's *Moses and Monotheism*, which I am reading in the cafe of the Austrian Hospice, a palatial building on the Via Dolorosa that was once the residence of the Austrian consul in Jerusalem. It is now a hostel for tourists and pilgrims in the Old City, with flights of clean stone steps and a little Viennese cafe.

Freud's theory is that Moses, the great architect of the Jewish religion, was not a Jew at all, but an Egyptian, a follower of Akhenaten, the pharaoh who had tried to impose an austere, ethically demanding monotheism on his own people. The Egyptians had turned against Akhenaten, and in due course the Jews likewise turned against Moses, murdering him. But later, driven by collective guilt, they invented the idea of a messiah, essentially Moses himself, who would return to save them. By this time they had merged with a Midianite tribe who worshipped the volcano god Jehova (a version of the thunder god Jove), and under the resurgence of longing for their lost father, they combined this choleric minor deity with the serenely omnipotent spirit that Moses had directed them to worship, thereby creating the hybrid God of the Old Testament: half ranting maniac, half celestial abstraction.

The book has been thoroughly discredited by historians (Freud too has joined the pantheon of tarnished names), but I find it extremely interesting – though possibly more for the curious difficulties involved in its composition than for its actual content.

Freud began writing it in Vienna during the thirties, under the protection of the Catholic Church. Hitler was chancellor in Germany, but in Austria the Church still appeared to be a bulwark of resistance against the Nazis. This put Freud in an awkward position, particularly concerning the second section of his book, where he develops ideas from his earlier work that consider religion in general as a mass psychological disorder.

'We are living here in a Catholic country under the protection of that Church,' he writes in the first of two prefaces to this section, 'uncertain how long the protection will last. So long as it does last I naturally hesitate to do anything that is bound to awaken the hostility of that Church.'

Self-censorship appeared to be his only option: the preface ends with a declaration that he has decided not to publish the essay. But then in 1938 the Nazis invaded Austria, and with the Catholic Church proving spineless after all, he fled to London: 'In the certainty of persecution – now not only because of my work, but also because of my "race", I left . . .'

The calamity was paradoxically liberating; you can feel his joy at the lifting of inhibitions in the second preface, which he wrote in London:

'I found the kindliest welcome in beautiful, free, generous England . . . I dare now to make public the last part of my essay.'

And yet even with the external obstacles removed, he was still troubled by what he called 'inner misgivings' and 'inner difficulties' with this book. He himself attributed these to uncertainty over whether he had amassed enough historical evidence to demonstrate how his analysis of religion in general applied to Judaism in particular. But this scholarly scruple doesn't convincingly account for the brooding self-doubt conveyed in this preface. 'The inner difficulties were not to be changed by the different political system and the new domicile. *Now as then I am uneasy when confronted with my own work . . .*' (my italics).

A likelier explanation becomes apparent in the text itself, where, in the course of discussing the psychology of anti-Semitism, Freud offers a number of observations on the special characteristics of Judaism and the Jewish people. The tone is respectful, even reverential, and there are moving evocations of the ethical grandeur and civilising force of the Mosaic vision (albeit undercut by the blasphemous earlier argument that Moses himself wasn't a Jew). But at the same time, the logic of his analysis forces Freud to say things that must have been uncomfortable for a Jew to say, or even think, at that particular moment in history, with the prospect of total extermination confronting his people.

For example, there is the comment that the Jewish religion was rendered, psychologically speaking, 'a fossil' by the advent of Christianity with its healthy recovery of repressed polytheistic impulses. Then there is the matter of the Jews' long-standing habit of cultural self-separation from their host societies, a subject that compels Freud to adopt, briefly but startlingly, the perspective of those societies at their most aggrieved: 'We may start with one character trait of the Jews which governs their relationship to other people. There is no doubt that they have a very good opinion of themselves, think themselves nobler, on a higher level, superior to the others . . .' And there is the final, triumphantly psychoanalytic unravelling of the ever-escalating asceticism that gives the adherents of this religion, at least the more orthodox ones, their special character. The passage begins admiringly enough: 'In a new transport of moral asceticism the Jews imposed on themselves constantly increasing instinctual renunciation, and thereby reached – at least in doctrine and precepts – ethical heights that had remained inaccessible to other peoples of antiquity . . .' But the conclusion is merciless: 'The origin, however, of these ethics in feelings of guilt, due to the repressed hostility to God, cannot be gainsaid. It bears the characteristic of being never concluded and never able to be concluded with which we are familiar in the reaction-formations of obsessional neurosis.'

One imagines that writing such things about the Jews in 1938, the year of Kristallnacht, must have given Freud – confident as he always was in the clinical impartiality of his own observations – some qualms. At any rate it seems fair to Freudianise the master here, and conjecture that there were strong unconscious reasons, beyond the immediate argument in hand, why considerations of ethics and guilt may have been on his mind, and why he was experiencing 'inner misgivings'.

But speaking of psychoanalysis, a comment that the archivist made at the V&A has been nagging at me.

I had put my father's hate letter in a pile of documents I was setting aside to copy. When the archivist saw it she gave a sort of sigh. 'Ah, that letter,' she said. 'Whoever wrote it was mentally ill. That's my opinion.'

At the time I'd thought nothing of it, but now I feel as if I was being gently reproved for digging up something sensationalistic for my article, some shameful relic that should have been left to decompose in peace.

My impulse is to jump to my own defence and assert that the writer of the letter was aware of what he was doing and that it was therefore perfectly appropriate to exhume it. But thinking back to the shouting capitals and thickly scrawled defacements, the hundreds of painstakingly inked-out lines of print, I become less certain. And I return to a question that has arisen periodically in my mind since Nasreen first began emailing me; namely, was Nasreen herself simply 'mentally ill', and if so is there any point, after all, in trying to write about her? Has her behaviour all along been just the chaotic by-product of chemical imbalances and misfiring synapses – to be regretted and pitied, surely, but in itself essentially meaningless?

I have mentioned the 'borderline' aspects, as they seemed to me, of Nasreen's personality. But I could probably have made the case that she was communicating from a place well and truly across the border. She herself seemed to want to convey that impression. Her emails contained dozens of references to her 'insanity', 'psychosis', 'nervous breakdowns', 'craziness', and so on, of which I have quoted only a fraction. There were those paranoid comments about mysterious forces tampering with her computer. And there was quite a bit of talk about doing drugs. Arguably, in other words, the whole saga could be explained purely and simply as some kind of 'mental illness', possibly worsened by drug abuse.

But I can't quite accept this. For one thing, 'mental illness' carries an implication that the sufferer isn't aware of the possible consequences of his or her actions and therefore shouldn't be held accountable for them. That seems reasonable in cases of real insanity, but however afflicted Nasreen may have been, she was obviously, calculatingly, tauntingly aware of the possible consequences of her actions, and by her own admission dead set on bringing at least some of them about ('I will ruin him'). For another, the very proclamations of her own 'insanity' seem precisely evidence that she was *not* insane, but rather that she was using the idea of insanity as leverage for manipulation.

Even as I write this, though, I am aware of the possibility of mixed motives in what I myself am doing. I have a strong vested interest, after all, in claiming that Nasreen was fundamentally sane. I want to hold her responsible for her behaviour. I tell myself that this is simply because I believe it to be the case, which I do. But I also have to admit that if I didn't, I would probably feel uncomfortable writing about her. Uncomfortable not only from a personal point of view but also from a literary one. As soon as you reduce human behaviour to a pathology – label it 'psychotic' or 'sociopathic', or attribute it to some kind of personality disorder – it becomes, for literary purposes, less interesting (at least to me). She's clinically this or that; she has X Syndrome, Y Disorder: well, maybe, but in that case there is no morally engaging antagonist and therefore, for me, no drama. Iago's 'motiveless malignancy', in Coleridge's famous phrase, brings the audience up against the mystery of evil with a force that would be seriously weakened if a psychiatrist were to appear in the play and explain his behaviour as the result of an excess of monoamine oxidase in his posterior cerebellum.

So I have reasons that may not be entirely objective for resisting a purely medical diagnosis of Nasreen's actions. But even as I acknowledge this, it occurs to me (and you could say this proves nothing except the urgency of my need to justify myself) that even if these outbursts – Nasreen's and that of my father's attacker – *are* instances of 'mental illness', they are perhaps not quite as special-case and narrowly applicable as I have been thinking. Might they not, on the contrary, be evidence of some naturally occurring feature in the human mind, one that by definition requires the presence of 'madness' in order to become observable, since, under present social conditions, nobody in their right mind would allow it to disclose itself?

The spasm-like, explosive nature of anti-Semitism, when you do witness it today, seems relevant to the conjecture. Often the outburst appears to be as startling to its perpetrator as anyone else, as if some constriction or inhibition had been unexpectedly lifted, some area of the psyche had come suddenly uncoupled from the social self with its diligent observance of proprieties and taboos. The look on the White House correspondent's face in the news footage after she has said that Jews should go back to Germany and Poland, for instance; a grimace of astonished horror, as if toads have just hopped out of her mouth. The extreme drunkenness involved in recent outbursts of anti-Semitism from fashion and movie celebrities. Even in its cooler, steelier form it seems to arise almost involuntarily in its perpetrators, insinuating itself into other impulses before its unmistakable fin surfaces. Moral outrage, for example, is the proper response to a news story of Israeli soldiers killing a Palestinian child, but when a poet writes of a Palestinian boy 'gunned down by the Zionist SS' you feel that something other than moral outrage has entered the picture: an opportunistic malice riding in on the wake of the legitimate disgust, itself having no particular interest in the child or the soldiers, but only the desire to seize a rare chance to call Jews Nazis. The tainted word 'Zionist' is the poet's alibi ('It's not Jews I'm against, only Zionists'), but his use of 'SS' as the slur of choice gives him away (imagine calling an African American soldier who killed a child a 'slave-trader' or a 'Klansman'). The urge to condemn people in their capacity as wrongdoers gives way mid-expression, mid-breath almost, to the apparently stronger urge to bait them in their capacity as Jews. The propensity for Judaism to keep drawing this kind of archaic lightning out of educated people even after the Holocaust seems an intrinsic part of its curious time-dissolving effect. Or put it this way: there is something uncannily adaptive about anti-Semitism: the way it can hide, unsuspected, in the most progressive minds.

In the early days of Israel, strictly Orthodox Jews were opposed to the Zionists. They rejected Zionism because of the Midrashic injunction not to hasten the will of God in creating a home for the Jewish people. The gap was narrowed somewhat by the teachings of the country's first chief rabbi, Avraham Kook, who held that the Zionists could be regarded as unconscious agents of God's will; their actions, whether they knew it or not, part of the divine plan to re-establish the House of David in Israel.

After Rabbi Avraham Kook died, his son, Rabbi Zvi Yehuda Kook, refined his father's theology, steadily aligning it with the politics of the young state. Some Orthodox groups continued to oppose the notion of a man-made state of Israel (some still do), but for Kook and his followers the earthly and the divine increasingly appeared to be on the same track. The final convergence came with the Six Day War. What more stunning evidence could there be of God's will than those lightning victories? To a religious mind, alert for signs in even the most mundane of occurrences, these seemingly miraculous events were proof of God's favourable disposition towards the Zionist project. 'The Almighty has his own political agenda according to which politics down here are conducted,' Kook jubilantly proclaimed. '. . . No earthly politics can supersede it.' Henceforth settlement of the Land of Israel was to be regarded as a divine commandment, a mitzvah. The Religious Settler movement was born.

Another member of the Kook family, Simcha HaCohen Kook, was appointed rabbi of the new Hurva synagogue a few months before my visit. The appointment was controversial, even within the Jewish Quarter. The head of the civic agency that oversaw the project (the Jewish Quarter Development Company) refused to attend the rabbi's investiture. I have been trying to arrange an interview with the rabbi for several days. The JQDC, who manage the synagogue, offered to put me in touch with him, but nothing has come of it so far. A few hours ago I walked down here to Hurva Square, where I am sitting now, to try my luck in person. A polite young man with a pistol took my number and told me someone would call soon, but I'm still waiting. It is Friday; soon Shabbat will have begun and Rabbi Kook won't be able to use a phone.

I am debating whether to pursue a line of thought in my article, concerning the philosophical implications of replicas. If you replicate the appearance of something, do you also replicate its meaning? Is this building in any meaningful way the 'same' as the Ottoman structure it replicates? If not, why not? At some point, if I were to go in this direction, I would bring in the Borges story about the writer who recreates *Don Quixote* word for word, not by copying it, but by immersing himself in the context of its original creation so thoroughly that he is able, as it were, to give birth to it a second time. Is it the same book, or do the same words magically mean something entirely different? From here my idea would be to move on to politics, specifically the topic of apartheid. If the outward features of South African apartheid evolve in another society, but do so by a different process and for different reasons than they did in South Africa, do they nevertheless mean the same thing and deserve to be called by the same name? Is the same visceral shunning reflex appropriate, or should criticism take account of the different underlying causes? Is it the case that while brutality and humiliation are what they are, regardless of underlying causes, there is nevertheless a difference between saying 'This is wrong' and 'This is apartheid'? That one is a legitimate moral reaction, while the other is a smear?

A gated lodge guards one main entrance of the synagogue and a locked stairway bars the other. Security is of course a serious matter in this city, but I have noticed that you can wander freely into the restored Sephardic synagogues down the road, whereas here visitors seem to be actively discouraged.

Perhaps it's just a literary prejudice of mine, but I seem to be developing a certain animosity towards this smooth, pale, architectural doppelgänger. Its gates and railings oppress the spirit. The sight of young men in black hats and business suits coming and going through side doors that are opened from the inside only after a knock, and then closed immediately behind them, adds an air of secretiveness to the overall effect. It doesn't help to learn, as I did this morning online, that one of the two donors who paid for the construction, a Ukrainian businessman, was reported by the FBI to have links with organised crime. (But perhaps that isn't true; perhaps he has his own Nasreen, smearing him on the Internet.)

The afternoon deepens and the streets begin to fill. Tourists and groups of Yeshiva students head towards the Western Wall. Locals are bustling about on last-minute errands before Shabbat begins. It also happens to be Rosh Hashanah, the Jewish New Year, so I imagine Rabbi Kook will be busy all weekend. And after that I return to the States.

I realise I left it rather late to start trying to get hold of him, and I'm wondering if this is because I don't really want to talk to him, and if so, whether this is because I am afraid that his views will resemble those of his illustrious relative Zvi Yehuda Kook, thereby necessitating a yet more uncomfortably treacherous-feeling attitude of hostility towards the synagogue than I already have, or the reverse: that he will be so moderate and sensible that my forebodings about the building, the vague sense I've been forming of it as some sort of cyclopic creature gazing broodingly at the Temple Mount with the unblinking eye of its dome, will prove frivolous and sensationalistic.

An hour passes. It doesn't look like I am going to hear from the rabbi. I get up from my bench and join the slow tide of figures moving towards the Western Wall. I was busy the previous Friday, and so today is also my last opportunity to do what I had planned to do: place myself at the Wall at sundown on Shabbat, and reflect.

There are families on their way to prayers now, the large families of the ultra-Orthodox, with six, eight, ten children – the fastest-growing religious group on the planet. What you notice about them as an outside observer is always their sheer extremity of self-differentiation, their physical unlikeness to any other group on earth.

Most traditional dress has a relationship to natural conditions that one grasps intuitively, even if one can't account in detail for specific features. But intuition alone will merely register the appearance of the Haredim as strange, and therefore at some level of consciousness estranging. Even to make the most basic sense of it you have to have educated yourself in some rather esoteric matters. The *shtreimel*, for instance, a wide cylindrical hat made of sable or of grey fox tails, the size and shape of an enormous cake, and very popular among the Jerusalem Ashkenazi, is a magnificent and yet unfathomably singular piece of Shabbat headgear, bearing no obvious kinship to any other hat. The fact that it is always worn over another head covering, the close-fitting yarmulke, further compounds the cryptic effect. If you know nothing of the traditions concerning its origin and symbolism – the decree forcing Jews to wear a tail on their heads, the conversion of an object of humiliation into one of dignity, the gematrial or numerological significance of the number of tails used and the relation of this to the tetragrammaton (the name of God), the special spiritual merit of wearing two head coverings, the allusion to the *shaatnez* rules from the Torah prohibiting certain uses of wool, the clockwise spiral wrapping of the fur to emulate and invoke the radiance of the Divine Presence, the overall intention to glorify not the wearer but the holiness of Shabbat – if you are ignorant of all this, you are likely to see the hat just as something at once disquietingly weird and unaccountably sumptuous, and find yourself wondering by what quirk of eccentric and extravagant self-regard a man would find it necessary to crown himself in this fashion. What it replaces, the tefillin, or phylacteries, worn on non-Shabbat days, is even more enigmatic. What is the uninformed eye to make of a black leather box strapped to the centre of a man's forehead like a miner's lamp shedding invisible light, another attached to his arm, facing inward to the heart, the leather straps wound and tied in precise arrangements unmistakably charged with meaning yet indecipherable by any process of natural deduction? Likewise with every other aspect of outward appearance: without a knowledge of the complex interplay of history and scripture, tsarist decree and Talmudic injunction, everything – the wigs and hairnets, the prevalence of silk, the mid-body *gartel* dividing the heart and mind from the sex organs, the uncut sidelocks, the right-over-left buttoning, the laceless Shabbat shoes, the satin *bekeshe,* or surcoat, that looks so lavish but is in fact intended to convey modesty, the knee breeches to avoid contact of clothing with the unclean ground, the fringed garments, and on, and on – everything is going to appear almost intentionally alien, uncanny, *unheimlich.* But even *with* this knowledge there remains, to the irreligious outsider, something unassimilable to one's instincts about human attire, a stubborn residue of mystery.

I remember another scene in the Singer novel. Changing planes in Rome, Shapiro notices the man in Orthodox garb he'd seen earlier on the flight from New York, this time with a group of young Yeshiva students in tow, all dressed like him. He stares at them as they wait for their connection to Tel Aviv. 'How did they become what they are?' he wonders, noting their indifference to the mocking glances of passers-by, the look of passion in their eyes, the air of eagerness to serve God, 'to carry out all His commandments and to assume even more rigors and restrictions . . .' He remembers a line from the Torah, the commandment to be other, different, *un*like: '"After the doings of the land of Egypt shall ye not do."' As Egypt changes its fads and fashions, he asserts, 'so must the true Jew constantly assume new rigors and restraints . . .' What Freud attributes to neurotically escalating Oedipal guilt at the murder of Moses, Shapiro explains as an arms race between worldliness and piety, one driving the other into ever more elaborate expressions of itself. His image of the soldier comes to me – *A soldier who serves an emperor has to have a uniform* – and I see these figures precisely as soldiers, though the volatile instability in my own point of view at once causes them to vacillate between that and Freud's counter-image of the descendants of a people racked by an unassuageable guilt that 'made them render their religious precepts ever and ever more strict, more exacting, but also more petty', and that pitiless observation of his: 'It bears the characteristic of being never concluded and never able to be concluded with which we are familiar in the reaction-formations of obsessional neurosis . . .'

Near the top of the steps leading down to the Western Wall Plaza, a vast, glass-encased golden menorah stands ready to be installed in the Third Temple when its hour comes round. 'May it be rebuilt speedily and in our days,' goes the legend on the sign below. It was created by the Temple Institute and paid for by one of the Hurva donors, the Ukrainian businessman with alleged links to organised crime. It used to be farther away from the Wall, in the Cardo, but it was recently moved forward, closer.

You can see the plaza from here; already milling with people, the density of the crowd increasing towards the bastion of the Wall itself. A man stands with his back to the steps, unwinding the tefillin from his left arm. His movements are exact, quietly ceremonious. There are elaborate rules covering every aspect of the manufacture and use of these objects, from the dyeing and stitching of the leather boxes to the tone of voice in which to recite the blessings while wearing them. The boxes contain verses from the Torah. They are worn, or 'laid', as a sign of remembrance – of God's hand leading the Jews out of Egypt – and they have also acquired the significance of a protective charm or amulet (the Greek 'phylakter' means 'guard'). They are not worn during the twenty-four hours of Shabbat because the period, being holy, is a sign and guard in itself. To wear them would be a blasphemy, a superfluous measure of self-protection that would imply doubt rather than faith.

Having duly removed them, the pious man proceeds on down the steps to present himself to the Almighty. Someone sounds a blast on a ram's horn shofar, summoning in the new year, which is also the Day of Judgement, and a volley of answering blasts goes off all around, echoing off the grey-gold cliff of the Western Wall.

I follow after him, passing through the security booth into the crowded esplanade. Closer to the Wall is a partition dividing the men's side from the much smaller women's area, but here at the back men and women, tourists and worshippers, mingle together. There is a carnival atmosphere, with the bleaty trumpeting of the shofars, and people calling out *shana tova*, the new year's greeting. Small groups merge into larger groups who hold hands in a ring and then splinter off haphazardly into singles again. Individuals tent a fringed shawl, a tallith, over their heads and conduct a private prayer service under it, each his own priest. There are teenagers, businessmen, tour groups, IDF soldiers in military fatigues and Shapiro/Freud's soldier-neurotics in their own regalia. They pray, chat, read, chant, stare entranced. In one corner of the plaza about eighty young men in white shirts, Yeshiva students, dance in a circle singing loudly, hands on one another's shoulders. Among them is an older, grey-bearded man with a large, handsome head tilted back in a way that makes the smile fixed on his powerful features seem superbly self-assured. There is something more concerted about this group than any of the others, a consciousness of their impact on the crowd around them.

I press on towards the Wall. Inside the men's section the nodding and chanting and davening are more concentrated. The crowd is thicker. Some men in fur *shtreimels* and silk stockings gather in front of me, talking in Brooklyn accents. Up close, the heavy masses of glistening fur have a dense materiality that for a moment blots out all thought of their religious or historical meaning, and I catch myself falling into my old, ignorant misprision of preening self-delight. Across the plaza the linked students uncouple and regroup in several short rows, one behind the other. Arms around one another's shoulders, they come towards the men's section in a half-marching, half-dancing shuffle. The grey-bearded man is at the centre of the front row, his smiling head thrown back as he leads his acolytes towards the Wall. All of them are smiling, in fact; their joy is palpable, and I am struck by the fact that this too, this dancing phalanx advancing on the Wall, is one of those images that can resonate with contradictory meanings depending on where you begin the story in which they appear. You could call it just a ceremonial crossing of empty space to a holy site. Or you could start earlier, when the plaza wasn't empty but comprised the old Moroccan Quarter with its houses crowding almost all the way up to the Wall, in which case you would have to describe how the Israelis tore down the houses immediately after the Six Day War, which would charge this empty space with meanings that might or might not trouble you but would certainly affect how you saw it and how you interpreted the dancing and marching impulses it seems to inspire. Or you could go back further, to the War of Independence, the final retreat of Jewish forces from the Old City following the destruction of the Hurva, which they were using as a stronghold, and the Jordanian commander's strange boast that 'for the first time in a thousand years not a single Jew remains in the Jewish Quarter. Not a single building remains intact. This makes the Jews' return here impossible', which would endow both space and dancing with yet another complexion. And so on.

A knock comes at the door. You let in the stranger, accept the challenge, venture forth, and a year later find yourself baring your own neck for the death blow of a freshly sharpened axe. The axe stalls in mid-air once, twice, but the third time it comes all the way down. To your astonished relief it does no more than very lightly nick your neck, spilling a little blood on the snowy ground.

New Year's Day – not the Jewish but the Christian New Year – is also the day of the climactic scene in *Gawain*, where the young knight finally re-encounters his nemesis. He wakes early and puts on his armour: the surcoat with its pentangle symbol of purity, but also the magic girdle, his not-so-pure charm against death, wrapping it twice around his waist. A man from the castle brings him as far as a tall cliff, where a path leads on to the Green Chapel, and leaves him there, afraid to go any closer. Alone, Gawain follows the path into a ravine under the cliff. There is nothing anywhere that looks like a chapel, only a smooth green mound off to the side. He rides over and sees that it is hollow; a grave mound or barrow, but empty, with entrances on four sides. *This*, he realises, is the Green Chapel, this stark hatchway between the worlds of the living and the dead. Suddenly he hears the sound of a blade being sharpened in the air above him: 'Quat! Hit clatered in the clyff . . .' The Green Knight is up there somewhere, hidden in the cliff like the *Shechina*, the Divine Presence, here in the Western Wall. But after a moment he emerges into plain sight, striding down towards Gawain, head squarely back on his shoulders.

He is Sir Bertilak, of course, and he carries the gigantic axe in his hand, ready to behead Gawain and finish the game he began a year earlier.

The two withheld blows are for the two evenings Gawain played true in the exchange of spoils, passing on the lady's kisses. As for the third, well, 'here yow lakked a lyttel, sir . . .' But it was just a token blow all the same: a little 'tappe', Sir Bertilak calls it, acknowledging that the girdle had been withheld from him, not for purposes of lecherous intrigue but out of a natural attachment to existence: 'Bot for ye lufed your lyfe . . .'

All this Sir Bertilak explains in great good humour under the cliff, laughing genially as he praises Gawain's generally commendable performance in the game, pressing him to keep the girdle as a souvenir of his adventure and assuring him that he is now fully absolved of all wrongdoing. He even invites him back to the castle to make up with the lady and meet the witch Morgan le Faye, Arthur's half-sister and Gawain's aunt. It was she, Sir Bertilak continues, thoroughly amused by it all, who dreamed up this whole beheading business in the first place, sending me to Camelot out of pure idle malice, to drive you out of your senses, 'your wyttes to reve'. But that's all water under the bridge as far as this indomitably jolly man is concerned, and there is no reason to dwell on any of it. Come back and say hello to your aunt, he entreats Gawain, as if after all nothing of any great consequence has occurred. 'Make myry in my hous . . .'

But Gawain isn't in the mood for making merry. Exposed in his little deceit, he is no longer able to ignore the gap between his impossibly pure image of himself and the flawed reality that has just been thrust in his face. Shame floods him, bitter and unassuageable. Fear taught me to forsake my nature: the largesse and loyalty that belongs to knights. Now am I faulty and false. There is no question of going back to the castle. As for the magic girdle (or not so magic, since he would apparently have been safer if he hadn't worn it), he will keep it, but only as the sign of his own guilt. Winding it carefully around his neck and shoulder, he laces it under his left arm, the knot against his heart, and sets off for Camelot, a newly minted soldier-neurotic from the dark ages, riding home to his fortress.

Laughter here too; jubilation at his safe return, but again he is unable to join in. Some terminal disenchantment has fallen over him. Like a time traveller from science fiction, he has journeyed too far and grown middle-aged in the space of a year. Haggard and brooding, he confesses everything to his old companions: displays the scar on his neck, shows them the girdle, his 'token of untrawthe', and declares his intention to wear it till his dying day. They listen but they don't understand what this self-flagellating gloom is about, and he can't seem to explain it to them. It's over, you're alive, any possible wrong you may have done you've more than atoned for; who cares about anything else? Irrepressible laughter surges back through the court. The king himself tries to cheer up Gawain. Someone has the merry idea that they should all lace a green girdle around themselves, and that henceforth it will be the Round Table's special symbol of honour and renown. And whatever pang of helpless exasperation or anguish this idea provokes in Gawain can only be imagined, because with that final image of a man forgiven everything by everyone but himself, indeed assured that there is nothing *to* forgive, the story ends.

Speaking for myself, though, nothing has ended and not much has changed, at least on the face of it. Nasreen's emails continue. I block the sender addresses, but new ones spring up in their place. Sometimes there are long periods of silence, sometimes the old rapid-fire bursts start up again. For a year or so the messages were more oblique, less overtly threatening, sometimes not even especially malicious at all. A while ago there was a link to a long, frankly confessional piece titled 'To Sir, With Love': 'I called him Sir because his father was knighted Sir by the English royal family as a carrot for the esteemed architecture the monarchy despised behind his back . . . Sir had lovely teeth, full lips, curly Jew-hair, a sexy amount of which peeked out of the collar of shirts that never were ironed. He looked disheveled, un-professorial and uber-professorial, all at the same time. I loved calling him Sir.' (Not that it matters, but a more objective eye would never have been able to discern much in the way of 'curly Jew-hair' on either my head or my chest.) 'My stalking of Sir began only a few days after I'd blindly sent out an unfinished manuscript of my novel-in-progress . . . Sir's former mistress, Elaine, made me fall in love with Sir. I fell in love with the way Sir saw me or the way Sir saw the female muse behind his writing, which Elaine made me believe is me and I wanted to believe is me (it is me!) . . .'

In May 2011 I went to Los Angeles to give a reading. It was advertised in the LA listings and Nasreen, who had been quiet for some time, went into a fresh frenzy of emailing. I knew she lived somewhere near LA, and as the day approached and her demands to know where I was staying started coming in, along with renewed protestations of love and hate and all the rest of it (including a mildly obscene photo of herself), I began to wonder if she was going to show up at the reading and stage some kind of incident.

The day before I was due to fly in happened to be the day Osama bin Laden was killed. Given Nasreen's identification with the spirit of terrorism (not to mention her assertion that I myself was 'the reason for terrorism'), I couldn't help feeling that this was a peculiarly fateful piece of timing, and at a certain point I realised I was going to have to warn the organisers of the reading about her. I called them up: 'Er, there's something I need to tell you . . .' I felt like the Ancient Mariner: doomed to tell his mad tale to every new stranger he encounters as he wanders the earth. I gave my reading under guard, with a security detail in the auditorium and the LAPD patrolling outside.

There have been tender words: 'i'm still in love. so much in love . . .'; an invitation to join her on a yoga retreat in Australia; some haunting cell phone photographs of little street scenes caught on the fly (sent to me as if I'd been temporarily recategorised from eternal enemy to dependably approving friend or mentor); even, in the spirit of Sir Bertilak inviting Gawain back to the castle as if nothing has happened, a social invitation: 'can we have coffee?'

But the old crazed hatred still persists. Recriminations about the unfinished novel: '**I want the full JEW treatment** . . . polish it . . . pretty it up you fucking animals'; demands for recompense for the 'theft' of her work: 'Pay me for it or I'll continue the music'; more Holocaust taunting: 'I wish Hitler had seen it through'; a link to Kate Bush singing 'James and the Cold Gun', with the lyrics helpfully typed out: 'You're a coward, James! You're running away from humanity . . .'

Since my visit to LA these *odi et amo* vacillations have grown increasingly elemental: 'James. I need you' one day; 'I want you banished from this earth' the next. She alludes to a new affair that seems to have gone wrong – 'he too is a rapist . . .' Her own family join the cast of villains: 'my brother, my father, my mother, my uncle and most of my siblings are SHIT.' Her self-presentation as the ultimate victim becomes ever more acidly emphatic: 'I'm just a dirty darky muslim girl . . .' while her inflated image of my standing in the world grows correspondingly surreal: 'Oh, but you love charity and to do super-star celebrity charity . . .'

Meanwhile the stain of defamation continues to spread. In the summer of 2011 Nasreen launched a Facebook campaign, trying to 'friend' people connected to me, and posting the full smouldering litany of accusations against me on various walls. Google entries under my name began to list links to these accusations, which now included having her drugged and raped at the national magazine where she'd worked. From Facebook she proceeded to the *Guardian*, where, in the online comments section under a book review I'd written, she posted:

```
Coming from James Lasdun, a mediocre writer himself,
whose last book is sexually sophomoric, I find this review
to be funny. At least the writer doesn't steal his
students' work and give it to others of the same
ethnicity. And, Mr. Lasdun, your own personal life is a
bad porn film and I'm sorry I didn't sleep with you and so
you had me raped and gave my work to AIPAC babies for $.
I see you're well connected at the Guardian. American
women would like you to move to England. —Nasreen, a
former student.
```

Other comments in the same vein followed. Unlike, say, my Wikipedia entry, *Guardian* articles and comments are seen by large numbers of people. 'Don't even try to repair your rep.,' she had written a couple of months earlier (I assume she meant 'reputation'), and at this point it did seem as if that tattered article was beyond repair. I hit the 'report' button, and the comments were quickly taken down, but I was badly shaken (in fact I was literally shaking). How long had they been up? How many others had been posted and taken down? What was to stop her from posting more? I write regularly for the *Guardian*: was I going to have to monitor my online pages around the clock? Or would I simply have to accept that this was now going to be a part of my life; that my public self, such as it is, was going to manifest this strange disfigurement wherever it appeared? If so, was there perhaps some different attitude I could acquire, some way of not minding about being publicly accused of rape and theft? Is such a thing humanly possible?

Abandoning her former caution, Nasreen now began making overt threats. Demands that I 'fix the fucking book' mingle with what appear to be dire warnings about what will happen if I don't: 'You are to blame for innocent deaths . . .'

She also began targeting my daughter, attempting to friend her on Facebook, warning me, 'your daughter is fucked', and proclaiming, 'I do voodoo. You'll see. She's going to go through fucking HELL for what you did to me . . .' When she informed me point-blank that 'your family's going to get it if you do not right your wrongs', I realised the time had come to call the police again. '**go call the cops . . .**' she wrote, ever clairvoyant, '. . . you get me in trouble and you're fucked. give me everything you have and go kill yourself . . .' I called the Albany FBI again (I had seen a notice on their website soliciting calls about Internet crimes) and was listened to politely, only to be instructed to contact a local field office instead, where an answering machine repeatedly informed me: 'This mailbox is full and not currently taking messages. Please try again later.' I left several urgent messages with Detective Bauer, but never heard back from him. Through Janice, however, I heard that he still didn't think the DA would extradite Nasreen, even for the more explicit threats she was now making. I had to wonder what it would take to stir that mighty personage into action. In desperation I called my local village police department, which I'd assumed wouldn't be able to do much about the situation. But they sprang into action, calling Nasreen immediately and warning her she would be arrested if she continued harassing me. I can't say I'm hopeful of any kind of long-term result (she has already broken her promise that she wouldn't contact me again), but it was reassuring just to be taken seriously.

It was Detective Bauer who had told me not to stop reading the emails in case they became violent enough to qualify as a felony. But if the bar for a felony was as impossibly high as it appeared to be, then what was the point of subjecting myself to the excruciating pain of reading the damn things? I began blocking them again, in-termittently; allowing myself the luxury of a few weeks' silence, before misgivings of one kind or another would get the better of me (might I have missed an allusion to some critically damaging Web posting or, worse, some crucial warning of impending violence?) and I reopened the channel.

On it goes, then; on and on and on. Supplications and impreca-tions flaring up and dying away like fevers of a recurrent illness. Threats, pranks with misappropriated email addresses (I opened one the other day from the British Council, hoping to find an invita-tion to some literary junket, only to read, under the official letter-head: 'your family is dead you ugly JEW'). Phone calls too, lately, with long obscene messages demanding money, promising to go on harassing me until I pay, telling my wife I slept with all my female students (except for Nasreen herself), all in a bizarre, unrecognis-able, sing-song voice, full of wearily narcotic allusions to the things

Jews do ('I *know* it's in the *Tor*ah, I know it's in the *Tal*mud, that you're supposed to rape Gentiles, steal from them . . .').

I try not to pay any more attention than I do to the midnight voices in my own head, which at times it closely resembles. Occasionally I lapse back into my old Inca torture agony, writhing prostrate on a sofa. More often, now that the saga has entered its fifth year and I have given up waiting for it to stop, I find myself simply wanting to make sense of it. Why is this happening? What does it mean? I want to understand this tormentor of mine who knows the workings of my mind so intricately and uses them so cleverly to make me suffer. I want, as St Augustine said, 'to comprehend my comprehender'. I want to know what she thinks she is doing. She must be aware, at some level, that I haven't stolen her work or sold it through some network of nefarious Jews to her literary rivals (she has never made any attempt to describe what it is she thinks these writers have stolen from her), that I didn't have her drugged and raped at the magazine where she worked. Why, then, is she devoting so much time and energy to making and pressing and elaborating these accusations? What happened – between us, or to her alone – to make my unremarkable existence matter so much to her?

A large part of understanding something is finding analogies for it. What is it like? What other situation does it resemble? For me, being who I am, the analogies that come to mind are most often from things I've read. *Gawain*, *Macbeth*, the Highsmith and Singer novels, Emily Dickinson's letters: all have seemed to shed some light. Lately I have also been looking at Sylvia Plath's poems, especially 'Lady Lazarus', that little tour de force of chortling malediction. It's a poem in the form of a piece of hate mail, after all (or so it seems to me now), complete with Nazified recipient: *Herr God, Herr Lucifer* . . . 'O my enemy. / Do I terrify?' Lady Lazarus asks this unlucky figure, and at once I hear Nasreen's mocking, menacing grandiosity. 'I am your opus,' Lady Lazarus declares (she seems to be on the

212

point of accusing her addressee of plagiarism); 'I am your valuable, / The pure gold baby . . .' And she too, in her search for ever more extreme terms to evoke her pain and fury, reaches for the Holocaust: her skin 'Bright as a Nazi lampshade', her face like 'Jew linen'.

What do I learn from these resemblances? Among other things, they force me to consider (given Plath's fate) the extremities of despair entailed in Nasreen's gleefully uninhibited aggression: its likely proximity to some unendurable pain. And this in turn, occasionally, causes me to feel compassion for her.

Or again: there is a recurrent gesture in classical mythology that might be termed the gesture of the offended woman. This consists of the splashing of water or some other liquid into the face of the offender, to drastic effect. Ceres, jeered at by a boy for drinking from her cup with unladylike gusto, spatters the boy with the brew, causing him to shrivel into a little wriggling-tailed lizard. When the hunter Actaeon stumbles on Diana bathing naked in a pool, the angry goddess splashes water at him, turning him into a stag (his dogs tear him to pieces). Proserpina flings water from the underworld river into the face of Ascalaphus when he reveals that she has violated the terms of her release from hell. The water turns him into a screech owl.

In my (crudely Freudian) reading of these stories, the liquid represents the state of female desire, aroused by attraction and then immediately weaponised by wounded pride; the men's crimes consisting, essentially, of an affront to sexual self-esteem, whether by mockery, clumsiness or betrayal.

In pagan terms, rejection of a woman's offer of love is a sin against nature, whose sole imperative is procreation, and it is always punished. There are stories that explicitly address that act of sexual rejection, and these have no need of the symbolic splashing (though you can feel how the symbol might have evolved from them: for instance, when the bashful youth Hermaphroditus rejects the advances of the nymph Salmacis in her pool, she deluges his naked limbs with her own in a watery embrace that merges their two bodies into one, creating the original hermaphrodite). I like the splash, though; the image it offers of elementally unbridled self-expression, the explosive manifestation of the goddess's inner core. For me this has connotations of extreme creativity as well as destructiveness. Both aspects seemed to me present in Nasreen's 'splash', the electronic tsunami she unleashed in response to what she saw as my offence. There was the pure destructiveness of the self-styled 'verbal terrorist'. But there was also something manifestly creative in her unstoppable productivity, a vitality I couldn't help envying.

Behind my constant sense of being up against the narrow limit of my own abilities is a vaguer, more intermittent sense of having possessed, at some point in the real or imaginary past, precisely an *abundance* of powers (I suspect many writers feel this). I began to think about that countervailing sense now. Was it just wishful thinking or did it have some basis in reality? If the latter, then how were such powers lost? Could they be destroyed by misuse? Forfeited because of something one had done or failed to do? Was there anything one could do to regain them? Dimly, certain ingrained habits of mine – decisions I had made, consciously or unconsciously; positions I had taken regarding this or that aspect of life or work – began to emerge out of memory and cluster around these questions, as if summoned for reappraisal.

What I am trying to express is that without being entirely aware of it, I had enlisted Nasreen as a guide to help me through the very crisis she herself had precipitated. Or at least my image of Nasreen, the real Nasreen bearing, I realised, no more resemblance to Diana or Ceres or Proserpina (or for that matter Lady Lazarus or Emily Dickinson or the Three Witches) than I myself do to Actaeon or Sir Gawain or Joseph Shapiro. But one way or another this shape-shifting, quasi-phantasmal being, veiled in her skeins of rage and madness, had become a part of my private navigational system; a *Fluchthelfer*, to use that word again, through what she had once, presciently (and in her own idiosyncratic fashion), referred to as my 'mid-life'. You could say I had stumbled on a way of deploying my own preferred form of resistance: weakness as strength; absorption of the blow rather than opposition to it. It didn't make the situation any better in practical terms, but it made it fractionally more bearable. It was certainly the only kind of resistance that did me any good.

And so here I am at the Wall. And naturally, having built it up in my mind as some kind of grand revelation-in-waiting, I am feeling suddenly a bit blank. The stones are impressive. The ones on the lower courses have frame-like indentations around them. They date from the time of Herod, when they formed the retaining wall under the Second Temple, destroyed in AD 70, after which the Jews went into exile. The ones above are plainer but equally massive. Weeds hang down here and there from the crevices, green and whiskery. I wonder idly if it would be in poor taste to describe them in my article as rabbinical-looking; if I could perhaps even bring in Gawain somehow, make a joke, Sir Gawain and the Green Rabbi . . . The truth is, I am not sure what I was expecting to find or feel or learn here.

Or no, that isn't quite the truth. I had actually planned to make this moment the climax of my amateur private investigation into the origins of anti-Semitism. With all due discomfort of self-exposure I was going to, as it were, lift the lid off my own brain here among these worshippers and find the little evil meme lurking there, the last unharried 'insult to mankind that exists in oneself' and make it, as Fanon said one must, 'explicit'.

But I don't seem to have the heart, or the appetite, or the courage, or whatever quality it would take, to complete this process of psychological auto-vivisection. It's possible that I simply don't possess the meme (though for professional reasons I hate to exempt myself from any human tendency, good or bad), and my half-formed theory of its physiological origin and consequent latent universality is fatally flawed. Or maybe it was just that those Brooklyn accents I heard earlier put me in mind of the other notorious remark made by the author of that 'Zionist SS' poem: that the Brooklyn-born settlers 'should be shot dead. I think they are Nazis, racists, I feel nothing but hatred for them . . .', and I am just recoiling in nausea from the whole exercise.

The poet is very sure that he is not an anti-Semite. An anti-Zionist, yes, and an opponent of Israel's right to exist, but not an anti-Semite. It seems to be important to him not to be thought of as anti-Semitic. People who have accused him of anti-Semitism are just playing the race card: 'They use this card of anti-Semitism. They fill newspapers with hate letters. They are useless people.' Nasreen also was sure that she was not anti-Semitic. 'I sound anti-semitic but I'm not,' she wrote in one email, and likewise it seemed important to her to discredit any accusation to the contrary.

Which raises the question of whether you can be an anti-Semite even if you categorically deny that you are one. Is it something you alone can decide that you are or aren't, like being a vegetarian, or is there something more involuntary about it, like a sexual orientation, which no amount of deciding or wishing or denying can change, and which may be clearer to others than it is to yourself? If the latter, then the next question might be whether society is going to continue to reject it or gradually accept it; in other words, whether it is going to go the way of paedophilia or of gay pride. If the latter, then . . . then what? The thought peters out before I can get to the end of it. I don't seem to be as interested in thinking about any of these questions as I had planned to be, now that I'm here.

And something is distracting me: an elderly man standing right up against the Wall, rocking on his heels and lost in what appears, from his half-turned face, to be a somewhat anguished state of prayer or supplication. He is wearing a plain grey yarmulke over his long, unkempt, not very clean-looking grey hair. His beard is matted and his coat is shabby in the extreme, brown and thread-bare, with torn pockets. He is the first genuinely down-and-out-looking person I have seen in Jerusalem, and I can't help wondering what his story could possibly be, and projecting all sorts of senti mental things onto him: Shapiro's piety, some kind of old-world shtetl simplicity, the outcast raggedness of the Wandering Jew him-self, until it occurs to me from a glimpse of rolling whiteness in his eyes as his head tips back (along with the very extreme nature of his swaying and moaning) that he is most likely just a bit cracked.

But what really interests me about him isn't the bowing and praying at all, but the fact that he is also engaged in screwing a little piece of balled-up paper into a chink between two stones. I realise I have been forgetting all about this aspect of the Wall, the thing that probably comes to mind before anything else for most people when they think about it: that it is a place where you come to post mes-sages to the Almighty.

Moving all the way up to it, I see that little folded or balled-up bits of paper have been crammed and jammed into every seam: not just the thin gaps between the stones but every crack and cranny in the stones themselves, and every pitted indentation on their surfaces. The accumulated scale and intensity of the little gesture is power-fully affecting; you feel the extreme urgency of the need to commu-nicate awoken by this sanctified and monumental surface.

On our last walk in Provence we climbed into the Mercantour wilderness, to see the Bronze Age rock inscriptions in the high val-leys under Mount Bego. Bego, it is conjectured, was a storm god and bull god, patron of the cattle-raising clans who lived there in the Bronze Age and covered the flat-faced boulders with their pictograms. A sign at the top of the trail points to the highest local concentration of the engravings, a sort of long, tilted wall of massive, glacier-polished stone tablets known as the Voie Sacrée, the Sacred Way.

I think of them now, those great, flat, sky-facing pages of rock, and the mysteriously communicative images their surfaces summoned from the hands of the cattle herders with their new bronze tools. Horns turning into daggers, daggers into lightning bolts. Figures brandishing axes. A bull's head tumbling. Storms drawn as thick stipplings in the orange-patinated schist. Meandering horns turning into rivers irrigating rectangular grids of pasture.

What are they all saying, those images, these balled-up texts here in the Western Wall? Nobody knows, but perhaps it isn't so hard to imagine. Send rain. Send love. I do love you and am in love with you. I'm sorry if I got screwy on you. You don't love me at all any more. Would you like to see me in a veil, sir? Your silence is scary, sir. You lack depth. You lack compassion. Say something. Give me your fucking keys. You pose as an intellectual but you're a corrupt thief. I am fond of you. I really am. Mr Horned God, so tacky. Fine, stay silent. I'm sorry if I've offended you. You need a garden full of me. Get a toupee. I'm sorry I've blamed you for so much. I want every cent. Old, shitty man! Two-faced psychotic. Give me everything you have. I'm still in love, so much in love. Can we have coffee?

And it's hard to know whether to be struck more by the conviction and energy of the effort, or by the tenacity of the silence surrounding it. Somehow they seem the measure of each other.